GENERAL MODULE

(Reading, Writing, Speaking & Listening Essentials)

Jyoti Malhotra
(B.A Hons. M.A., NET-1, E-Commerce)

V&S PUBLISHERS

Published by:

F-2/16, Ansari road, Daryaganj, New Delhi-110002
☎ 23240026, 23240027 • *Fax:* 011-23240028
info@vspublishers.com • www.vspublishers.com

 **Online Brandstore: amazon.in/vspublishers**

Regional Office : Hyderabad
5-1-707/1, Brij Bhawan (Beside Central Bank of India Lane)
Bank Street, Koti, Hyderabad - 500 095
☎ 040-24737290
vspublishershyd@gmail.com

Follow us on:   

BUY OUR BOOKS FROM: AMAZON FLIPKART

ISBN 978-93-505712-8-6
New Edition

Printed at : Param Offsetters, Okhla, New Delhi–110020

Dedication

I, with due respect and profound privilege, serene dignity and folded hands dedicate my small piece of research program to my devoted and dedicated parents, Mrs. Kiran Malhotra and Mr. Pradeep Malhotra for their wholesome support and their dignified ambience which they offered me to sail the boat of my life on the path of hardwork and determination. I am really very thankful to both of them for blooming my life with their humble ambience.

Acknowledgement

There is a big vote bank of thanks in my whole projection of this project to my worthy parents, Mrs. & Mr. Deep Birla, My Guide, Mr. Parminder Singh Bhogal, Caring Brothers & Sisters - Mrs. & Mr. Rohit Gandhi, Mrs. & Mr. Aman Malhotra and Mrs. & Mr. Sandeep Malhotra.

My heartiest thanks to my life partner, Mr. Deepak Malhotra (husband) and the little steps of my Angel, Ditya Malhotra (daughter).

I am really grateful to be a part of the V & S Publishers who support my research analysis with their expert team of publishing. I am really very thankful to Mr. Sahil Gupta (Director) and Mr. Binay Srivastava for their wholesome cooperation to convert my research program to a complete masterpiece.

Regards

Jyoti Malhotra

Publisher's Note

V&S Publishers has recently ventured into the field of *Academic Books* with the launch of the *Gen X Series*. 'Gen X' stands for 'Excellence in Generation 'X'. The series comprises books for aspirants of various competitive examinations. Hence, following the success of our previous books in this series, we decided to launch a **series of IELTS or the International English Language Testing System books** under this series. The subject has been divided into five main parts which has been grouped into five books by the author, such as: ***IELTS Tech-Academic Module***, ***IELTS Tech-Writing Essentials***, ***IELTS Tech-Vocal Cosmetics***, ***IELTS Tech- General Module*** and ***IELTS Tech- Speaking Essentials*** for the students, who aspire to study, work or settle abroad.

The books in this exclusive Series are written especially for the Indian students who wish to appear in the IELTS exams. Most of the foreign books available in the market on this subject have been written keeping in view the foreign readers and at times, may appear *Greek* to the students from India, primarily because of issues related to accent, grammatical aspects, spellings, etc. Therefore, the need for these books was felt by V&S Publishers and the author's extensive research on this subject was carefully moulded to present it in the form of five perfect books on IELTS, specifically for Indian students.

Each book contains **Skills, Strategies and Guidelines** written in a simple manner. Unique feature of this book is additional content accompanied with the book, available online on dropbox: https://www.dropbox.com/sh/yl50pqjye86wiwm/AABCQK1Z6v88v0L6hbYW8Amka?dl=0. The content here is **interactive and illustrative** and presented in a manner that even an average student can grasp the contents and master the language easily and quickly. V&S Publishers hopes that through these books, we can offer the IELTS aspirants--**A Smarter Way to Learn Technical English nationwide.**

Scan Dropbox QR Code : 

Contents

Listening Module

Preface

IELTS- TECH - A complete Toolkit for learning, practising and knowing about IELTS. As the world is growing smarter, the ways of its learning and getting education also gets smarter day by day. IELTS-TECH (A TECHNICAL TOOLKIT OF LEARNING INTERNATIONAL LANGUAGE TESTING SYSTEM) is also acting as a smarter way to learn IELTS via Presentations on its strategies. This toolkit completely clarifies four sections.

Reading:

This refers to the IELTS aspirants' development in reading, understanding and responding to a wide range of spoken, written and visual English texts. It involves learners' developing understandings of how texts are organised and how language varies according to the situation, social and cultural contexts, purpose and audience.

Writing:

It refers to the IELTS aspirants' development in writing a range of texts for interpersonal, informational and aesthetic purposes. It involves developing writing skills including task response, Coherence, Lexical Resource and Grammar skills

Speaking:

This refers the IELTS aspirants' development in using spoken Standard English for communication for social and school-based learning. It involves developing learners' control over Standard English phonology, word and sentence stress, rhythm and intonation and the information conveyed by these systems.

Listening:

It refers to the IELTS aspirants' development in understanding spoken Standard English. It focusses on the ability to actively listen for a purpose and involves learners being able to select and apply strategies to make meaning in a wide range of contexts.

IELTS TECH SERVES THE YOUNG ASPIRANTS WITH ITS TOOLKIT OF FIVE BOOKS

BOOK 1 : IELTS -Tech : It includes Reading, Writing, Speaking, and Listening along with its strategies to crack with the practice sessions.

BOOK 2 : WRITING ESSENTIALS : It will serve the Academic and General candidates with writing topics. This book covers the wide range of Graphical Representation, General letters and few Academic and General topics of writing.

BOOK 3 : VOCAL COSMETICS AND SPEECH THERAPY FOR IELTS: This book will enhance the speaking skills of the candidate. Students will come to know the technical aspect in IELTS related to speaking techniques like Word Stress, Intonation, Rhythm, Coherence, Lexical Resource, Fluency, etc.

BOOK 4 : GENERAL MODULE FOR IELTS This book will help the general candidate who are appearing for IELTS. It covers Reading, Writing, Speaking and Listening skills with strategies and practice sessions.

BOOK 5 : SPEAKING ESSENTIALS : This will serve both the Academic and General candidates regarding interview sessions between interviewer and interviewee. It covers PART-1 Personal Interaction, PART-2 Cue -Cards, PART-3 Follow up Session.

SPECIAL ATTRACTION IN IELTS – TECH

AWARENESS SESSIONS : These powerpoint smart sessions will help the students to build their ideology towards simple topics like Education, Media, Music, Technology, Tourism, Culture, Science, Computers, Health, etc. These awareness sessions is an endeavour to raise the standards of vocabulary and terminology of the aspirants. This will enhance the lexical resource for Writing and Speaking skills. These awareness sessions not only serves Vocabulary Usage but also provides Traditional and Contemporary Outlook, Quotations and Proverbial Matter, Author Sayings, Volley of Idioms and Phrases related to it… etc. Ancillary content (Uploaded on Dropbox) will be provided with the Writing Essentials and Speaking Essentials books.

ADDITIONAL SMART CONTENT OF POWERPOINT PRESENTATION ON DROPBOX : IELTS- TECH is a smart tech product which help the aspirants to understand the technicalities of the IELTS exams with visual aids. This product is the package of strategies to crack the four modules of IELTS, i.e., Reading, Writing, Speaking and Listening with its Do's and Don'ts.

ONLINE CONTENT ON DROPBOX FOR LISTENING SESSIONS: For enhancing the listening part of the candidate, listening activities are provided online on Dropbox for their practice.

ABSTRACT
READING MODULE

The IELTS Reading Test has three sections which require 60 minutes to complete the test. For this, it is essential for the IELTS candidates to know the skimming & scanning technique to improve their band score in the reading test. This chapter completely discusses the exact format, strategies and techniques to solve the IELTS Reading Test, Marking Scheme and Question Types.

Chapter 1 : Reading Strategies and Skills

The Test Format

The IELTS General Training Reading Test has 3 sections. You have 60 minutes to complete the test. There is NO extra time at the end of the test to transfer your answers to the answer paper (you get 10 extra minutes in the listening test only); your answers must be on the answer paper at the end of the 60 minutes. The test has 40 questions based on a series of texts. The total length of all the texts put together should be between 2000 and 2750 words. As in all the different parts of IELTS, the *IELTS General Training Reading Test* gets progressively harder through the paper. Possible formats of texts could be: *notices, advertisements, newspapers, instruction manuals, leaflets, timetables, books and magazines*.

Section 1

Section 1 will normally have 2 or maybe 3 'texts' with 13 or maybe 14 questions to answer in 2 or 3 sets of differing formats. We will look at the types of questions that you will meet later. Section 1 tests the candidate on 'social survival' in an English speaking country. The questions usually involve the candidate finding and providing factual information from a variety of texts. Texts in section 1 are relatively short and there may be a number of 'mini texts' to look through, eg: a series of advertisements on similar subjects.

Section 2

Section 2 again usually has 2 texts with 13 or maybe 14 questions to answer. Section 2 concentrates on the context of training and welfare in an English speaking country. The texts here are more complicated using more intricate language and structure.

Section 3

Section 3 has 1 text with 13 or maybe 14 questions to answer. Section 3 tests candidates' ability to deal with longer pieces of writing. The reading passage will again involve more complex language than the 2 previous sections.

Marking

There are 40 questions in the IELTS General Training Reading Test and 1 mark is awarded for each correct answer. There are no half marks. Your final marks out of 40 is then converted to a band from 1 - 9 using a converting table and this band is then averaged with the other 3 parts of the test to give your final IELTS band.

The IELTS General Training Reading Test Marks, Bands and Results - Rough Guide Converter

Score	Band
1 - 2	1
3 - 5	2
6 - 11	3
12 - 17	4
18 - 25	5
26 - 33	6
34 - 37	7
38 - 39	8
40	9

Question Types

Below is a list of the types of questions that you could meet in the IELTS General Training Reading Test.

- ✯ Multiple Choice Questions
- ✯ Short Answer Questions
- ✯ Completion Questions: Completing Sentences
- ✯ Completing Notes
- ✯ Completing a Summary (no word bank)
- ✯ Completing a Summary (with word bank)
- ✯ Completing a Diagram
- ✯ Completing a Flow Chart
- ✯ Completing a Table
- ✯ Matching a Bank of Headings to Identify Paragraphs or Parts of Text
- ✯ Matching a Bank of Writers' Views/Claims/Information with the Writer
- ✯ Identification of Information in the Text: Yes/No/Not Given Questions

- ✯ True/False/Not Given Questions
- ✯ Matching Lists/Phrases
- ✯ Classification Questions

Some Tips for the IELTS General Training Reading Test

1. Don't spend too long on a single question as that will lose you time for answering questions that could be easier for you. Sometimes, leaving a question and coming back later can help you answer it too. Leave any questions that you have spent too long on, and come back at the end of the test if you have time. Sometimes, if the question has a yes/no/not given answer, the answer you are looking for does not exist as it could be a not given one. Be aware so you don't waste time looking for something that isn't there.

2. Read the questions and instructions so that you don't make a silly mistake. For example, people often will mix the yes/no answers with the true/false answers and write yes as an answer instead of 'true' or vice versa. Strictly speaking, you are wrong although you have understood the question and answer.

3. If the question asks for one answer, then give one answer. Giving two is wrong as it asks for one and you will be marked wrong. The type of question where this could happen would be: Give one example of... Writing two examples, to show you really understand, is wrong.

4. If the question asks for no more than 3 words, use no more than 3 words. Writing 4 words or more is wrong. You won't be asked to do it in 3 words or less, unless it is possible. Therefore, don't worry; it can always be done.

5. One area that students don't like is that, in the Reading Test, good grammar and spellings are important. The grammar part is not as important as you can't make many grammar errors in 3 words (the maximum you use in the reading test) but, if you spell something wrong, it will be marked as wrong. People think, quite rightly in my opinion, that the reading should test whether you understand what you read and not how you spell something. But these are the rules. So, be careful about your spellings too!

6. One constant discussion we have had with students is whether to read the questions first and then read the passage, or read the passage first and then the questions. From our experience with our students, my conclusion is that there is no correct answer for this. It depends on a number of variables.

   It can depend on the types of questions and how difficult the questions are. It can depend on how good and fast a reader you are. It can also depend on the length of the text and how much time you have. Let's look at these variables.

Various Variables

1. If the question type is difficult and asking something which is hard to answer, then reading the text first can help. Just a quick read through using a technique called *skimming* can give you the knowledge of the text that will help you find the answers more easily.

2. If you are a good, fast reader, then you can read the text quickly, getting good knowledge of the contents without using too much of your precious time. This can help you answer the questions better.

3. If the texts are short, then it doesn't take long to quickly read through them. On the other hand, if the texts are short, it is easier to find the answers so you may not have to waste time reading the texts to find the answers quickly, especially if the time is short.

4. If the time is short, then it doesn't matter how complex or long the texts are. You need to get some answers on the answer sheet as quickly as possible. So, you can see that there is not one answer to the problem of whether to read the texts or questions first.

5. Time management is an important thing to be aware of. You have a number of texts to read and 40 questions to answer in 1 hour. If you spend too long on one part, you may find that you have not enough time to finish all the questions and some of those questions could be ones that you could answer quite easily. As I said above, don't spend too long on a difficult answer, but also keep an eye on the clock. It's a good idea to have your watch or a small clock on your desk so you know exactly how long you have left in the test at any given time. In addition to this, keep a control on how long you spend on each section.

Remember the IELTS General Training Reading Test gets more difficult as it goes on, so you will probably need more time for the questions at the end than for those at the beginning. Maybe a guideline could be:

17 minutes on section 1.

20 minutes on section 2.

23 minutes on section 3.

Reading Techniques - Skimming and Scanning

Skimming and scanning are the two main techniques that people use to read and answer the IELTS Reading Tests. It's not a question of using one or the other, but you will need both methods in doing the test. Let's have a look at the two techniques in turn.

Skimming

Skimming is reading fast to get the 'gist' or the *general idea of the text*. There are different techniques of doing skimming.

1. You can run your eyes over the text getting the general meaning, not stopping at words that you don't understand as this will slow you down. The important thing with skimming is *speed.*

2. Another way to skim is to just read the first and last paragraphs of a text and the summaries as well.

3. You could also just read the title, subtitles and illustrations if there are any. For IELTS the first way – reading it all quickly to get the general meaning, but of course it depends on your reading speed. If you are a slow reader in English, you really need to practise to improve.You can practise with any English texts, but, nearer the exam, you should do your practice on the IELTS Practice Tests.

Scanning

This is another very important technique for the IELTS Reading Tests. This is the technique that you use when you are reading a telephone book or a dictionary. You are not starting at the top and reading every line back and forth as you would read a novel.

You are moving your eyes around the text, back and across and up and down. You are searching for some specific information: a word or name. This is an important technique in IELTS reading as you are often searching for some specific information. You read the question and then you search for the key words or ideas associated with the question.

READING PRACTICE TEST 1

SECTION - 1

Questions 1 - 9

CAUSTON HEALTH CENTRE PATIENT INFORMATION LEAFLET

A. Appointments

Please telephone 826969 (8.30am - 5.00pm: Mon - Fri). We suggest that you try to see the same doctor whenever possible because it is helpful for both you and your doctor to know each other well. We try hard to keep our appointments running on time, and ask you to be punctual to help us achieve this; if you cannot keep an appointment, please phone and let us know as soon as possible, so that it can be used for someone else. Please try to avoid evening appointments if possible. Each appointment is for one person only. Please ask for a longer appointment if you need some more time.

B. Weekends and Nights

Please telephone 823307 and a recorded message will give you the number of the doctor from the Centre on duty. Please remember this is in addition to our normal working day. Urgent calls only please. A Saturday morning emergency surgery is available between 9.30am and 10.00am. Please telephone for home visits before 10.00am at weekends.

C. Centre Nurses

Ms. Reena, Ms. Anita and Ms. Alley are available daily by appointment to help you with dressings, ear syringing, children's immunisations, removal of stitches and blood tests. They will also advise on foreign travel, and can administer various injections and blood pressure checks. For any over 75s unable to attend the clinic, Ms. Alley will make a home visit. AII three Centre Nurses are available during normal working hours to carry out health checks on patients who have been on doctors' lists for 3 years.

D. New Patients

Within 3 months of registering with the Centre, new patients on regular medication are invited to attend a health check with their doctor. Other patients can arrange to be seen by one of the Centre Nurses.

E. Services Not Covered

Some services are not covered by the Centre e.g. private certificates, insurance, driving and sports medicals, passport signatures, school medicals and prescriptions for foreign travel. There are recommended fees for these set by the National Medical Association. Please ask at reception.

F. Receptionists

Our receptionists provide your primary point of contact-they are all very experienced and have a lot of basic information at their fingertips. They will be able to answer many of your initial queries and also act as a link with the rest of the team. They may request brief details of your symptoms or illnesses which enables the doctors to assess the degree of urgency.

G. Change of Address

Please remember to let us know if you decide to relocate. It is also useful for us to have a record of your telephone number.

Questions 10-14

BENTLEY HOSPITAL CATERING SERVICE

TO ALL PERMANENT AND TEMPORARY MEMBERS OF THE STAFF

Important Information

Meal Breaks (minimum company guidelines)	
Hours worked	Break to be taken
0-4 hrs	nil
4-6 hrs	15 mins
6-8 hrs	30 mins
8-12 hrs	60 mins (taken as 2 x 30 mins)
12-24 hrs	75 mins (taken as 2 x 30 mins + 1 x 15 mins)

Your section staffing board will show the times when these breaks are to be taken.

Please note

It is your responsibility to check that the total break time shown on the staffing sheets accurately reflects the breaks that you take. Any discrepancies should be raised with your Staff Coordinator immediately.

Special Requirements - Food Handlers

Food handlers are those concerned with preparing and serving unwrapped food.

Food handlers should report any instance of sickness, diarrhoea and/or stomach upset experienced either while at work or during a holiday to a member of the Personnel Management team. Any infections of ear, nose, throat, mouth, chest or skin should also be reported to a member of the Personnel Management team.

Food handlers need to have an annual dental examination by the company dentist. Alternatively, a current certificate of dental fitness may be produced from their own dentist. This applies to all permanent staff who handle food.

Questions 1-4

Reading Passage 1 has seven sections, A-G.

Which paragraph contains the following information?

Write the correct letter, A-G in boxes 1-4 on your answer sheet.

1. What to do if you need help outside normal working hours?
2. Who to speak to first for general information?
3. What happens when you register with the Centre?
4. What to do if you need to cancel a doctor's appointment?

Questions 5-9

Do the following statements agree with the information given in the Reading Passage 1?

In boxes, 5-9 on your answer sheet, write:

True	*if the statement agrees with the information*
False	*if the statement contradicts with the information*
Not Given	*if there is no information on this*

5. You must always see the same doctor if you visit the Centre.
6. If you want a repeat prescription, you must make an appointment.
7. Helen Stranger is the Head Nurse.
8. It is possible that receptionists will ask you to explain your problem.
9. You should give the Health Centre your new contact details, if you move house.

Questions 10-14

Complete each sentence with the correct ending, A-J, below.

Write the correct letter, A-J, in boxes, 10-14 on your answer sheet.

10. Temporary employees only working 3 hours should

11. Employees who work 11 hours should

12. To find out when to have their breaks, employees should

13. Employees working with food must

14. Food handlers who have been ill

A. talk to a staff coordinator.

B. have two thirty-minute breaks.

C. not take any breaks for meals.

D. pay for any meals they have.

E. get a single one-hour break.

F. look at the section staffing board.

G. lose pay for their break times.

H. tell a member of the Personnel Management team.

I. have an annual dental examination.

J. consult their doctor.

SECTION- 2

Questions 15-21

HAMPTON COLLEGE INTERNATIONAL SCHOLARSHIPS

There are seven types of scholarships offered by the Hampton College to enroll international students to assist with the costs of their courses. With the exception of applications for scholarship category E, all newly-enrolled international students are automatically considered for these scholarships. The scholarship is awarded in the student's first year as a credit to the second semester course fees. In all subsequent years, the scholarship is awarded as a credit to the first semester course fees. The scholarships are awarded once a year unless otherwise stated.

The scholarship categories are:

A. One scholarship of $2000 for the most outstanding students entering the Foundation Studies Program from each of the following countries: Singapore, Malaysia and Thailand. An additional six scholarships are available for students from other countries. These scholarships are offered on two dates to students in the March and June intakes of the program. Scholarships are awarded on the basis of first semester results.

B. Three scholarships providing 25% of the course fees for the duration of the course to the 3 most outstanding *State Certificate of Education* (SCE) students entering a Diploma or Certificate program. Scholarships are awarded on the basis of the previous year's SCE results.

C. Seventeen scholarships providing 25% of the course fees for the duration of the course to the outstanding Diploma or Certificate students entering each Hampton College School: three each in the Schools of Business and Engineering; two in the School of Applied Science; two in the School of Environmental Design and Construction; two in the School of Art and Design; two in the School of Social Sciences and Communications; one in the School of Biomedical and Health Science; one in the School of Education and one in the School of Nursing. Scholarships are awarded on the basis of the first semester results.

D. One scholarship of $4000 per annum for the duration of the course to the most outstanding student entering the Diploma in Communication. Scholarships are awarded on the basis of the first semester results.

E. Nine scholarships of $3000 per annum for the duration of the course to the most outstanding students commencing any Advanced Certificate course. Scholarships are awarded on the basis of the Basic Certificate results (not the SCE results). Note that applicants need to apply for this scholarship on the Hampton College International Scholarship Application Form.

F. One full-fee scholarship to the most outstanding student commencing a Diploma in Art and Design (Photography) course. This scholarship is offered every second year, and is awarded on the basis of the results obtained in the Certificate in Design course.

G. Four half-fee scholarships to the outstanding students of the Hampton College's Singapore campus for the final year of the two-year Certificate in Business Studies to be completed in Melbourne, Australia. Scholarships are awarded on the basis of the first year results.

Questions 22-27

USING THE INTERNET AND THE CD-ROM DATABASES IN THE LIBRARY

The Hampton College now has full electronic information resources in the College Library to help you in your studies. On the CD-ROM in the library, we have about 50 databases, including many statistical sources. Want to know the average rainfall in Tokyo or the biggest export earner of Vanuatu? It's easy to find out. Whether you are in the School of Business or the School of Art & Design, it's all here for you.

You can conduct your own CD-ROM search for no charge, and you can print out your results on the library printers using your library photocopying card. Alternatively, you can download your results to disk, again for no charge, but bring your own formatted floppy disk or CD-ROM. If you are not sure how to conduct a search for yourself, the library staff can do it for you, but we charge $20 for this service, no matter how long or how short a time it takes.

All library workstations have broadband access to the Internet, so you can find the web-based information you need quickly and easily. If you are unfamiliar with using the Internet, help is available in several ways. You can start with the online tutorial Netstart; just click on the 'Netstart' Icon on the Main Menu. The tutorial will take you through the basic steps to using the Internet, at any time convenient to you. If you prefer, ask one of the librarians for internet advice (best at quiet times between 9.00am and 11.30am weekdays) or attend one of the introductory group sessions that are held in the first two weeks of each term. Sign your name on the list on the Library Bulletin Board to guarantee a place, as they are very popular.

A word of warning: demand for access to library workstations is very high, so you are strongly advised to book a workstation, and you have to limit your use to a maximum of one hour at any one time. Make your booking (for which you will receive a receipt) at the information Desk or at the enquiry desks in the Media Services Area (Level 1). Also, the use of the computers is limited to the Hampton students only, so you may be asked to produce your Student Identification Card to make a booking, or while using the workstations.

Questions 15-21

Reading Passage 2 has six sections, A-G.

Which paragraph contains the following information?

Write the correct letter A-G in boxes, 15-21 on your answer sheet.

NB You may use any letter more than once.

15. It is awarded on results obtained in the SCE exam.

16. It is only available to students from the College's overseas branch.

17. It is not offered every year.

18. Students need to apply for it.

19. It is offered twice each year.

20. It pays 100% of the student's tuition fees.

21. It provides 50% of one year's fees.

Questions 22-27

Choose the correct Ietter A, B, C or D.

Write the correct letter in boxes, 22-27 on your answer sheet.

22. To use the library printers, students must have:

A. a floppy disk.

B. correct change in coins.

C. a photocopying card.

D. their own paper.

23. To copy search results to a floppy disk, students pay:

A. $20.

B. no fees.

C. a fee based on actual costs.

D. a fee dependent on the time taken.

24. If the library staff, searches for information on the CD-ROM, students pay:

A. $20.

B. no fees.

C. a fee based on the actual costs.

D. a fee dependent on the time taken.

25. Students can learn to use the Internet:

A. at all times.

B. in the first two weeks of the term only.

C. Monday to Friday only.

D. between 9.00am and 11.30am only.

26. To ensure efficient access to the library workstations, students should:

A. queue to use a workstation in the Media Services Area.

B. reserve a time to use a workstation.

C. work in groups on one workstation.

D. conduct as many searches as possible at one time.

27. At any one time, students may use a library workstation for:

A. half an hour.

B. one hour.

C. two hours.

D. an unlimited time.

SECTION- 3

Questions 28-40

THE WATER CRISIS

Greater efficiency in water use is needed to meet the growing demands of a changing world

A. The per capita water usage has been on an upward trend for many years. As countries industrialise and their citizens become more and more prosperous, their individual water usage increases rapidly. Annual per capita water withdrawals in the USA, for example, are about 1,700 cubic metres, four times the level in China and 50 times the level in Ethiopia. In the 21st century, the world's limited supply of renewable freshwater is trying to meet the demands of both larger total population and increased per capita consumption. The only practicable ways to resolve this problem in the longer term are economic pricing in conjunction with conservation measures.

B. Agriculture consumes about 70% of the world's freshwater, so improvements in irrigation can make the greatest impact. At present, the average efficiency in the use of irrigated water in agriculture may be as low as 50%. Simple changes could improve the rate substantially, though it is unrealistic to expect very high levels of water-use efficiency in many developing countries, faced as they are with a chronic lack of capital and a largely untrained rural workforce. After agriculture, the industry sector is the second biggest user of water and, in terms of value added per litre used, is 60 times more productive than agriculture. However, some industrial processes use vast amounts of water. For example, production of *1 kg of aluminium might require 1,500 litres of water. Paper production too is often very water-intensive.* Though new processes have greatly reduced consumption, there is still plenty of room for big savings in the industrial uses of water.

C. In rich countries, water consumption has gradually been slowed down by price increases and the use of modern technology and recycling. In the USA, industrial production has risen fourfold since 1950, while water consumption has fallen by more than a third. Japan and Germany have similarly improved their use of water in manufacturing processes. The Japanese industry, for example, now recycles more than 75% of the processed water. However, industrial water consumption is continuing to increase sharply in the developing countries like india. With domestic and agricultural demands also increasing, the capacity of water supply systems is also under growing strain.

D. Many experts believe that the best way to counter this trend is to impose water charges based on the real cost of supplies. This would provide a powerful incentive for consumers to introduce *water-saving processes and recycling*. Few governments charge realistic prices for water, especially to the farmers. Even in rich California, farmers get water for less than a tenth of the cost of supply. In many developing countries, there is virtually no charge for irrigation water, while energy prices are heavily subsidised too (which means that farmers can afford to run water pumps day and night). Water, which was once regarded as a free gift from heaven, is becoming a commodity, which must be bought and sold on the open market just like oil. In the oil industry, the price increases which hit the market in the 1970s, coupled with concerns that supplies were running low, led to new energy conservation measures all over the world. It was realised that investing in new sources was a far more costly option than improving efficiency of use. A similar emphasis on conservation will be the best and cheapest option for *bridging the gap between water supply and demand.*

E. One way to cut back on water consumption *is simply to prevent leaks*. It is estimated that in some of the biggest cities of the Third World, more than half of the water entering the system is lost through leaks in pipes, dripping taps and broken installations. Even in the UK, losses were estimated at 25% in the early 1990s because of the failure to maintain the antiquated water supply infrastructure. In addition, huge quantities of water are consumed because used water from sewage pipes, storm drains and factories is merely flushed away and discharged into rivers or the seas. The modern approach, however, is to see the used water as a resource which can be put to good use – either in irrigation or, after careful treatment, as recycled domestic water. Israel, for instance, has spent heavily on used water treatment. Soon, treated, recycled water will account for most of the farm irrigation there. There are ether examples in cities, such as St Petersburg, Florida, where all municipal water is recycled back into domestic systems.

F. Another way of conserving water resources involves better management of the environment generally. Interference with the ecosystem can have a severe effect on both the local rainfall patterns and the water run-off. Forest clearings associated with India's Kabini Dam project reduced the local rainfall by 25%, a phenomenon observed in various other parts of the world where large-scale deforestation has taken place. Grass and other vegetation act as a sponge which absorb rainfall, both in the plants and a round. Removal of the vegetation means that the rainfall runs off the top of the land, accelerating erosion instead of being gradually fed into the soil to renew groundwater.

G. *Global warming* is bound to affect the rainfall patterns, though there is considerable disagreement about its precise effects. But it is likely that as sea levels rise, countries in low-lying coastal areas will be hit by the seawater penetration of groundwater.

Other countries will experience changes in rainfall which could have a major impact on the agricultural yield – either for better or for worse. In broad terms, it is thought that rainfall zones will shift northwards, adding to the water deficit in Africa, the Middle East and the Mediterranean - a grim prospect indeed.

Questions 28-34

Reading Passage 3 has seven paragraphs, A-G.

Choose the correct heading for each paragraph from the list of headings below:

Write the correct number i-x, in boxes 28-34 on your answer sheet.

List of Headings

- (i) American water withdrawal
- (ii) Economic pricing
- (iii) What the future holds
- (iv) Successful measures taken by some
- (v) The role of research
- (vi) The thirsty sectors
- (vii) Ways of reducing waste
- (viii) Interdependence of natural resources
- (ix) The demands of development
- (x) The consequences of agriculture

28. Paragraph A

29. Paragraph B

30. Paragraph C

31. Paragraph D

32. Paragraph E

33. Paragraph F

34. Paragraph G

Questions 35-40

Complete the summary below.

Choose NO MORE THAN TWO WORDS from the text for each answer.

Write your answers in boxes, 35-40 on your answer sheet.

Individual water usage is rising dramatically as people living in industrialised countries become increasingly

35. .... As well as increased consumption per capita, the growing demand for fresh water is due to a bigger global

36. .... than in the past. The only way to control this increase in demand is to charge high prices for water while also promoting conservation measures. Improvements in irrigation systems and industrial processes could dramatically increase the efficiency of water use. There are examples of industries in some rich countries that have reduced their consumption rates through price increases, the application of

37. .... and recycling. But in agricultural and domestic sectors, the price of water is still subsidised so it is not regarded as a commodity that people need to pay a realistic price for.

Other ways of protecting supplies are to reduce water loss resulting from

38. .... in the supply systems and to find ways of utilising used water. Longer term measures, such as improved environmental

39. .... would protect the ecosystem and ensure the replenishment of ground water for future generations. Without such measures, future supplies are uncertain, especially when global warming is expected to interfere with rainfall patterns and to worsen the

40. .... already suffered by many countries today.

Reading Practice Test 1

Answers

1. B
2. F
3. D
4. A
5. False
6. Notgiven
7. Not given
8. True
9. True
10. C
11. B
12. F
13. I
14. H
15. B
16. G
17. F
18. E
19. A
20. F
21. G
22. C
23. B
24. A
25. A
26. B
27. B
28. ix
29. vi
30. iv
31. ii
32. vii
33. viii
34. iii
35. Prosperous
36. Population
37. Modern Technology
38. Leaks
39. Management
40. Water deficit

READING PRACTICE TEST 2

SECTION 1

Read the information below and answer the questions (1-14) on your answer sheet

SELF-CATERING HOLIDAY COTTAGES IN THE LAKE DISTRICT NATIONAL PARK

At Lilliput Farm, we have three cottages for rent as self-catering holiday accommodation.

We have been awarded 4 stars in the Holiday Accommodation Accreditation Service for excellence in quality and service.

Dairymaid's Loft is situated above the barn under the eaves. It is the largest of the properties, having one double bedroom with en suite, a twin room and a single room. There is also a sofa-bed in the living room. There is a large kitchen, a living room, a dining room and newly-fitted bathroom. Please note that, since the entire property is on the first floor, and the stairs are steep, the accommodation is not suitable for the elderly, the infirm, the pets and the very young children.

The Shepherd's Rest is suitable for up to four occupants. There is a double bedroom and a twin room with bunk-beds. There is a small kitchen and a large living room. There is a shower room with separate WC. The accommodation is spread over two floors. Pets are allowed, but we request that they are kept downstairs.

The Haymaker's Den is a one-bedroom cottage at the ground floor level. There is also a sofa-bed in the living room which can sleep two people. It has a large living area comprising a kitchen/dinner and a living space. There is a ramp leading up to the property, and the large bathroom is fitted so as to be suitable for wheelchair users and people who use walking aids. We ask that pets are not brought into this property.

All the properties have: a television, a CD player and a DVD player. Dairymaid's Loft and Haymaker's Den have Sky Television. Shepherd's Rest has wi-fi access. Cots can be provided to all properties, but please note that Dairymaid's Loft may be unsuitable for toddlers and crawling babies. All properties have a washing machine, fridge freezer and microwave. Dairymaid's Loft also has a dishwasher and a tumble drier.

The cottages share an outside area with swings, a patio and barbecue area. Outdoor furniture is available in the barn.

All cottages have electric power. None are fitted with gas. Electricity is paid via a meter. You will receive a £10 worth of electricity at the beginning of your stay with our compliments (£5 for short breaks). After that, you will need to add money to the meter. Shepherd's Rest also has a wood-burning stove. Guests will receive one complimentary basket of wood. Subsequent baskets can be purchased for £2 each. Please help yourself to the woods in the barn and put money in the honesty box.

Cottages can be booked by the week or for short breaks. Short breaks are either on Fridays – Mondays (3 nights), or Mondays to Fridays (4 nights). Discounts are available in the low season (October to March). Couples staying in Dairymaid's Loft and Shepherd's Rest can also get a 2 percent discount. Week-long bookings are on a Saturday – Saturday basis. We regret that it is not possible to accommodate arrivals on Fridays. We ask that guests arrive after 3pm and vacate the property by 10.30 on their departure date, so allow us to clean and prepare the properties for the next guests.

To make a booking, you will need to make a deposit of 50 percent up front. The remainder is payable one month before your arrival. (If you make a booking less than a month in advance, you must pay the entire amount up front). If you need to cancel your stay, you will receive a complete refund if you contact us 30 days in advance of your booking. Cancellations made two weeks in advance will receive a 60% discount. We regret that we cannot give a discount for cancellations made less than two weeks in advance.

Select the following dcns to fill the following blanks from (1-6). You can use hints more than once.

Hints:- Haymaker's Den, Shepherd's Rest, Dairy maid loft

1. Which of the cottages is most suitable for the following guests?

   An elderly couple, one of whom uses a walking frame? ....

2. A family of two adults and two children, the youngest being 3 years old? ....
3. A group of six young adults ....
4. Someone who wants to use the internet during their stay ....
5. Someone who doesn't want to wash up while on holiday.
6. A family with a dog ....

Do the following statements (7-10) agree with the information given in the passage?

True	-	*if the statement agrees with the information*
False	-	*if the statement contradicts with the information*
Not Given	-	*if there is no information on this*

7. Guests have to pay extra for all the electricity they use ....

8. Each property has its own garden. ....

9. Dairymaid's Loft costs less to rent if only two people stay there in December. ....

10. There are no electric heaters in Shepherd's Rest. ....

Complete the spaces (11-14) using no more than three words or a number.

11. Guests staying for a weekend should arrive on a ....

12. Guests staying for a full week should arrive on a ....

13. If you book two weeks before your stay, you must pay .... % of the cost at once.

14. To get all your money back, you must cancel your stay at least .... in advance.

SECTION - 2

Read the information about visas for entry into the UK and then answer the questions.

BORDER REGULATIONS AND VISA APPLICATIONS

If you wish to come to the United Kingdom, either as a visitor or a student, you may need to apply for a visa. Visas vary according to your age, the length of your stay and your level of English study.

The following visa types are available:

A. Child Student

B. Child Visitor

C. Adult Student

D. Student Visitor

E. Prospective Student

The UK operates a points-based system which will decide whether or not you can apply for a visa. You need 40 points in order to apply for a visa. You will obtain 30 points if you have confirmation from the college, university or school that you have been accepted on a course. Your chosen place of studies must be registered on the UK Border Agency list of sponsors. You can obtain a list by clicking on the link below.

You will need to earn a further 10 by demonstrating that you cover the cost of your study fees and living costs. In doing so, you can be rest assured that you will avoid financial difficulties while you are studying.

If you wish to extend your study experience in the UK, you will need to pass a further points-based assessment to ensure that you have been accepted on another course and that you can afford to pay the fees and living costs.

To make your UK study experience even richer, you may be eligible for a work and study visa. Getting a job while you are studying can improve your language skills and enhance your CV by showing that you are flexible, team-oriented and well-organised. You will also be able to get a reference from your employer which will help you gain employment in the future. Before accepting a job, you must find out whether your visa allows you to work in the UK, and the maximum number of hours you can work each week from the UK Border Agency. Most UK places of study have a career service which will help you to access job listings, write a CV or application form and prepare for a job interview.

To work in the UK, you will need a *National Insurance Number*. This number is used to deduct money from your earnings to fund benefits for the unemployed, incapacitated and the retired. To obtain a National Insurance Number, you will need to attend an Interview. You can make an appointment for an interview by calling 0845 600 0643 during usual office hours. You will need to take the proof of identity, proof of your right to work in the UK and written proof of your job offer. You may start work before your number is issued as long as your employer deducts the appropriate national insurance contributions from your pay.

Each of the short paragraphs below gives information about the five types of visas, A-E. Read each paragraph and choose which of the five links would contain this information. There is one paragraph that you do not need.

A. Paragraph i. If you have already completed a course of study in the UK and do not intend to study further, you can apply for this visa to extend your stay. This visa allows you to work in the UK for a further 6 months.

B. Paragraph ii. If you are under the age of 17 and wish to study for less than six months, you can apply for this visa. If you wish to extend your course of study, you may not swap to a student visa, while you are in the UK. You must return to your home country and do so there.

C. Paragraph iii. Students in post-16 education can apply for this visa. This visa is suitable for students attending courses for over six months. Holders of this visa may be eligible to work in the UK.

D. Paragraph iv. Students over the age of 18, who wish to study for up to six months can apply for this visa. This visa does not allow students to work in the UK. Students may only extend their visa or switch to a student visa by returning to their home country.

E. Paragraph v. You can apply for this visa, if you are between the ages of 4 and 15 and intend to attend a full-time, fee-paying independent school for a period of over six months or more. 16 and 17 year olds may attend part-time, fee-paying establishments.

F. Paragraph vi. If you want to come to the UK before choosing your course of study, you can apply for this visa. You will need to start your course within 6 months of arrival. You may switch to an adult or child student visa, while in the UK without returning to your home country.

Select the paragraph (i-vi) to fill the following blanks (15-19) on your answer sheet.

15. Child Student ....

16. Child Visitor ....

17. Adult Student..............................

18. Student Visitor...........................

19. Prospective Student..........................

Choose the appropriate option which fulfils the criteria of the written statement and answer the following blanks from (20 -25) on your answer sheet.

20. You can obtain 30 points towards your visa if..............................

21. If you want to extend your study visa... ....

22. You can work in the UK if..................................

23. For advice on finding a job, the writer suggests that you contact ....

24. Your national insurance number will ensure that...............

25. You can start work ....

SECTION - 3

Scouts are arranged in different age groups. The youngest section of the Scouts is for the Beaver Scouts. The Beaver Scout organization accepts members between six and eight years old, and engages them in a 'Balanced Programme' which is intended to encourage socialization and self-discovery. The Beaver Scouts are encouraged to develop creativity and practical skills while finding out more about the world around them and developing a knowledge of the beliefs and attitudes of others. It is intended that they should complete the programme and be ready to move to the Cub Scout programme when they are eight years to eight years six months old.

The basic idea behind the Beaver Scout programme is that young people can develop themselves and have fun at the same time. The Beaver Scouts are encouraged to share and work on cooperative projects, and are taught the value of helping others. Playing games and listening to stories are essential parts of the course, and the Beaver Scouts are given the chance to try their talents at making things, acting, singing or making music. The Beaver Scouts usually meet once a week in a Beaver Scout colony, and sometimes, they participate in organized sleepovers - which are sometimes, the first time that they have spent a night away from home without their parents.

A. Awards and Badges

The Beaver Scouts wear a distinctive turquoise sweatshirt which displays the badges and awards that the scout has earned. Though emphasis is on giving the children the broad experience of the Balanced Programme, badges and awards are still a vital part of scouting. There are several different classes of badges.

B. Joining in and Group Badges

These are often rectangular. Group badges are generally worn on the right sleeve, or sometimes, displayed on the back of the Scout's scarf. Joining in badges are worn on the left of the chest and reflect how long an individual has been associated with the Scout Movement, and the yellow moving on award is given when the Scout moves to a new level – for example from the Beaver to the Cub.

C. Activity Badges

Activity Badges are circular and worn on the other sleeve to group the badges. Gaining activity badges is optional, but they show that the Beaver Scout has learnt a skill or particular understanding of an issue. Activity badges include Healthy Eating, where Scouts have to prepare a healthy snack, list some unhealthy foods and be able to make wholesome sandwiches and fruit salads. Earning a Faith Badge includes writing a prayer or a reflection on spiritual matters and visiting a place of worship. There are a dozens of these badges, as well as staged activity badges which show the level the Scout has reached in things like information technology, swimming or first aid.

D. Challenge Badges

Challenge Badges are diamond-shaped and are worn on the other side of the chest from Joining in Badges. Unlike Activity badges, Challenges are a part of the Balanced Programme, and the Scouts can earn badges for the Outdoor Challenge, the Discovery challenge and the Friendship Challenge. If a Scout is particularly interested in a particular challenge; that challenge can be completed more than once to earn a second badge, but to get the second badge, the scout has to show greater skills and knowledge of the topic.

E. Awards

Above the Challenge Badges, a Scout displays any awards for the meritous conduct or gallantry. This includes the oval-shaped Chief Scout's Bronze Award which is the highest award available in the Beaver Scout Section. This is gained by completing the Outdoor challenge, one of the other challenges and a personal challenge. (The personal challenge might be, for example, earning a certificate gained through swimming, gymnastics, ballet or music.)

26. Which is the most appropriate title for section A?

a. How to become a Beaver Scout?

b. About Beaver Scouts

c. Learning about Practical Skills

d. The Beaver Scout Message

Decide from the information in the text whether these statements are true, false or if the information is not given.

True	*if the statement agrees with the information*
False	*if the statement contradicts with the information*
Not Given	*if there is no information on this*

27. An essential part of the course is acting, singing and making music.

28. Sleepovers happen at the Beaver Scout Colony.

29. Learning about themselves and other people are objectives of the course.

30. Discovering socialism is encouraged.

31. Scouts must choose to earn either Challenge or Activity Badges.

32. All Beaver Scouts participate in the Balanced Programme.

Write the letter which indicates where the badges for the following achievements would be worn.

(You do not need all the letters, and you can use some letters more than once.)

33. Becoming a member of a part of the Scouting Organization

34. Doing something, particularly Brave or deserving of recognition

35. Getting a badge for completing the Outdoor and Personal and Discovery challenges

36. Learning how to use a Computer

37. Completing the Personal and Friendship Challenges

38. Beaver Scouts teaches:

a) the value of helping others.

b) the value of cooperative projects.

c) sharing & playing.

d) All of these.

39. The Sweat Shirt of Beaver scouts displays:

a) their experience.

b) their participation.

c) their talent.

d) their badges & awards.

40. The Shapes of Badges are:

a) rectangular.

b) square.

c) circular.

d) hexagonal.

Reading Practice Test 2

Answers

1. Haymaker's Den	21. V
2. Shepherd's Rest	22. ii
3. Dairy maid's loft	23. i
4. Shepherd's Rest	24. Vii
5. Dairy maid's loft	25. Viii
6. Shepherd's Rest	26. B
7. False	27. False
8. False	28. Not given
9. True	29. True
10. Not given	30. False
11. Friday	31. False
12. Saturday	32. True
13. 100	33. D
14. 30 days	34. C
15. Paragraph v	35. C
16. Paragraph ii	36. E
17. Paragragh iii	37. A
18. Paragraph iv	38. A
19. Paragraph vi	39. B
20. Xi	40. A

READING PRACTICE TEST 3

SECTION- 1

Australian Immigrant Investor Visa Details and Online Application Form

Questions 1-7

MAIL ORDER BROCHURE

Want some great clothing ideas for your family?

Our key for clothing specials in July:

M for men W for women C for children

For under $ 10

Cotton socks C- made of pure cotton for long wearing

Woollen socks C- to keep young feet warm in winter

Sports socks M- to go with jeans and other casual clothes

Patterned belts W- to go with jeans and other casual clothes

For under $ 25

Cotton shirts W- for day and evening wear

Silk shirts M- five sizes, in designer colours, for that special social occasion

T shirts C- hard-wearing, white with a variety of animal motifs

Colour T-shirts M W- cotton and polyester blend, plain colours, no ironing

For under $ 50

Blue jeans M W- non-shrink, colourfast, small sizes only

Silk shirts M W- plain and patterned, all sizes

Hooded jacket C- protects from the wind, 4 sizes, large strong pockets

jacket W- waterproof with zipper front, all sizes

☆ ***Or you can buy a gift voucher so that someone else can choose. These come in $10, $20 and $50 amounts.***

Additional monthly specials for July to September

July- $10 voucher with any purchase over $60

August- Travel alarm clock worth $19.95 free with purchases of $80 or more!

September- Children's backpacks. Free with any credit card purchase over $75!

Note: *Postage and packing charges*

These are applied to each order as follows:

Within Australia:

$7.95 per address, regular post

$17.95 for Express Delivery Service (overnight)

OVERSEAS

Surface Mail (allow a minimum of two months for delivery)

Airmail (allow around two weeks delivery to most destinations)

Questions 8-14

New Book Releases

A. This book describes the creativity of the Aboriginal people living in the driest parts of Australia. Stunning reproductions of paintings, beautiful photography and informative text.

B. Pocket-sized maps and illustrations with detailed information on the nesting sites and migration patterns of Australia. This is a classic booklet suitable for both the beginner and the expert.

C. Packed full of information for the avid hiker, this book is a must. Photographs, maps and practical advice will guide your journeys on foot through the forests of the southern continent.

D. More than an Atlas – this book contains maps, photographs and an abundance of information on the land and climate of countries from around the globe.

E. Australia's premier mountain biking guidebook – taking you through a host of national parks and state forests.

F. Here's the A-Z of Australian native animals - take an in-depth look at their lives and characteristics, through fantastic photographs and informative text.

G. Graphic artists have worked with researchers and scientists to illustrate how these prehistoric animals lived and died on the Australian continent.

H. A definitive handbook on outdoor safety with a specific focus on equipment, nutrition, first aid, special clothing and bush skills.

I. Detailed guides to 15 scenic car tours that will take you onto fascinating wilderness tracks and along routes that you could otherwise have missed.

SECTION 1

Question 1-14

Questions 1-7

Do the following statements agree with the information given in the text.

In boxes, 1-7 on your answer sheet, write:

True	*if the statement agrees with the information*
False	*if the statement contradicts with the information*
Not Given	*if there is no information on this*

1. Women's cotton socks cost less than men's.
2. Men's silk shirts are available in more than five colours.
3. Children's 7-shirts come in a variety of colours.
4. The child's jacket has four pockets.
5. If you buy clothes worth $80 in August, you will receive a free alarm clock.
6. The charge for special next-day delivery in Australia is $7.95.
7. All clothings is guaranteed to arrive within two months.

Questions 8-14

The list of New Book Releases on the following page has nine book descriptions A-I.

Choose the correct title for each book from the list of the book titles given below. Write the correct number (i-xi) in boxes (8-14) on your answer sheet.

List of Book Titles

i. Field Guide to Native Birds of Australia

ii. The Bush on Two Wheels: 100 Top Rides

iii. Bush Foods of Australian Aborigines

iv. A Pictorial History of the Dinosaur in Australia

v. Bushwalking in Australia
vi. World Geographica
vii. Driving Adventures for 4-wheel-drive Vehicles
viii. Survival Techniques in the Wild
ix. Encyclopaedia of Australian Wildlife
x. Guide to the Art of the Australian Desert
xi. Field Guide to Animals of the World

8. Book A

9. Book B

10. Book C

Example **Book D** **Answer vi**

11. Book E

12. Book F

13. Book G

14. Book H

Example **Book I** **Answer vii**

SECTION-2

Questions 15-20

WORK & TRAVEL USA

Do you want to heve the best summer holiday ever?

Have you just graduated and want to escape for a unique experience abroad?

Only $1950 will make It all happen!

This unbeatable program fee includes:

- ★ return flight from Sydney to Los Angeles (onward travel in USA not included)
- ★ 3 months' insurance cover
- ★ 2 nights' accommodation on arrival plus meet and greet and airport transfer
- ★ arrival orientation by experienced InterExchange staff
- ★ visa application fees

You also have:

- ★ access to a J 1 visa enabling you to work in the USA
- ★ an extensive directory of employers
- ★ InterExchange support throughout the program
- ★ 24-hour emergency support throughout the length of the program

Call toll-free 1800 678 738

InterExchange has 50 years' experience in international student exchange programs. 18,000 students from around the world travel yearly to the USA on this very program. InterExchange con also offer you work opportunities in other countries.

What is Interexchange?

InterExchange, one of the world's leading operators of international exchange programs and related services:

- ★ is a non-profit, non-governmental organisation
- ★ has 700 professional staff in 30 countries worldwide
- ★ was founded in 1947

InterExchange operates these programs for students all around the world. It offers you trained and travelled staff, plus full support during the application process. You can choose any job that interests you anywhere in the USA, whether that is working in a law firm in Boston, a famous ski resort in Colorado or serving coffee and doughnuts in the buzzing streets of New York. You can select the period you work and the period you travel; you may want to work for 1 month and travel for 3, or work the entire duration of your stay. The choice is yours.

You can Take up this Opportunity if you Are:

- a full-time student at an Australian university or TAFE college
- presently enrolled, or finishing this year, or you have deferred a year of study
- over 18 years old by November in the academic year in which you apply to the InterExchange
- enthusiastic about the experience of a lifetime ...

Questions 21-27

Contents: Arthur Phillip College

A about Arthur Phillip College	**G** learning methods
B entry requirements	**H** course fees
C orientation for new students	**I** study commitment
D academic counselling service	**J** assessment and results
B credit courses to university	**K** social activities and clubs
F assistance for international students	**L** what's new

SECTION-2

Questions 15-27

Questions 15-20

Do the following statements agree with the information given in the advertisement.

In boxes, 15-20 on your answer sheet, write

True	*if the statement agrees with the information*
False	*if the statement contradicts with the information*
Not Given	*if there is no information on this*

15. The program cost includes internal flights within the USA ________________.

16. Emergency assistance offered in the program includes legal advice________________.

17. InterExchange offers similar programs in countries other than the USA ____________.

18. InterExchange is part of a government program ____________.

19. There are no restrictions on the type of job you can do ____________.

20. There is an upper age limit for applicants ____________.

Questions 21-27

Each of the short paragraphs below (21-27) gives information about Arthur Phillip College.

Read each paragraph and choose which of the linked sections of the website, A-L, would contain this information.

Write the correct letter, A-L in boxes (21-27) on your answer sheet.

21. All students receive a transcript of results and relevant award documentation when they end their studies with the College ____________.

22. On enrolment, all students receive an automatic membership to the Social Club and Public Speaking Club. Students may choose to participate in any arranged activities. The College encourages and promotes interaction between students and the teaching and the non-teaching staff ____________.

23. Successful completion and the achievement of an A or B result in some courses will enable students to achieve advanced standing in these subjects if they proceed to university study. For a list of the courses acceptable to a particular university, e-mail us your request with the name of the university and the course you are interested in ____________.

24. Arthur Phillip College is one of the top business colleges in Sydney, Australia. The College offers a wide range of educational and training programs in business and related areas. Its accredited vocational training courses are designed to meet the needs of individual students and industry ____________.

25. At Arthur Phillip College, you will learn from lectures, seminars, case studies, group projects, individual assignments and class workshops. Lectures and seminars present concepts and ideas and provide for question-and-answer sessions. Students are expected to take an active role in the learning process through class participation, presentations and projects ____________.

26. Courses at Arthur Phillip College involve an average of 25 hours per week of tuition time, with supervised group study accounting for a further 5 hours per week. At least 10 hours per week of individual study is also recommended for most courses ____________.

27. During this program, you will meet the Director of Studies, teachers and key administrative staff such, as the Accommodation Officer and Student Counsellor so that, right from your first day, you will know how each of them can help you during your time at the College ________________________________.

SECTION- 3

Questions 28-40

LACK OF SLEEP

Section A

It is estimated that the average man or woman needs seven-and-a-half to eight hours' sleep at night. Some can manage a lot less. Baroness Thatcher, for example, was reported to be able to get only four hours' sleep a night when she was the Prime Minister of Britain. Dr Jill Wilkinson, senior lecturer in psychology at the Surrey University and co-author of 'Psychology in Counselling and Therapeutic Practice', states that healthy individuals sleeping less than five hours or even as little as two hours in every 24 hours are rare, but represent a sizeable minority.

Section B

The latest beliefs are that the main purposes of sleep are to enable the body to rest and replenish, allowing time for repairs to take place and for the tissues to be regenerated. One supporting piece of evidence for this rest-and¬repair theory is that production of the growth hormone somatotropin, which helps tissue to regenerate, peaks while we are asleep. Lack of sleep, however, can compromise the immune system, muddle thinking, cause depression, promote anxiety and encourage irritability.

Section C

Researchers in San Diego deprived a group of men of sleep between Sam and Lam on just one night, and found that levels of their bodies' natural defences against viral infections had fallen significantly when measured the following morning. 'Sleep is essential for our physical and emotional well-being and there are few aspects of daily living that are not disrupted by the lack of it', says Professor William Regelson of the Virginia University, a specialist in insomnia. 'As it can seriously undermine the functioning of the immune system, sufferers are vulnerable to infection.'

Section D

For many people, lack of sleep is rarely a matter of choice. Some have problems getting to sleep, others with staying asleep until the morning. Despite popular belief that sleep is one long event, research shows that, in an average night, there are five stages of sleep and four cycles, during which the sequence of stages is repeated.

In the first light phase, the heart rate and the blood pressure go down and the muscles relax. In the next two stages, sleep gets progressively deeper. In stage four, usually reached after an hour, the slumber is so deep that, if awoken, the sleeper would be confused and disorientated. It is in this phase that sleep-walking can occur, with an average episode lasting not more than 15 minutes. In the fifth stage, the Rapid Eye Movement (REM) stage, the heartbeat quickly gets back to the normal levels, and the brain activity accelerates to daytime heights and above and the eyes move constantly beneath the closed lids as if the sleeper is looking at something. During this stage, the body is almost paralysed. This REM phase is also the time when we dream.

Section E

Sleeping patterns change with age, which is why many people over 60 develop insomnia. In America, that age group consumes almost half the sleep medication on the market. One theory for the age-related change is that it is due to hormonal changes. The temperature General Training: Reading and Writing rise occurs at daybreak in the young, but at three or four in the morning in the elderly. Age aside, it is estimated that roughly one in three people suffer some kind of sleep disturbance. Causes can be anything from pregnancy and stress to alcohol and heart disease. Smoking is a known handicap to sleep, with one survey showing that ex-smokers go to sleep in 18 minutes rather than their earlier average of 52 minutes.

Section F

Apart from, the *self-help therapy,* such as regular exercise, there are psychological treatments, including relaxation training and therapy aimed at getting rid of pre-sleep worries and anxieties. There is also *sleep reduction therapy*, where the aim is to improve sleep quality by strictly regulating the time people go to bed and when they get up. Medication is regarded by many as a last resort and often takes the form of sleeping pills, normally benzodiazepines, which are minor tranquilizers.

Section G

Professor Regelson advocates the use of *melatonin* for treating *sleep disorders*. Melatonin is a naturally secreted hormone, located in the pineal gland deep inside the brain. The main function of the hormone is to control the body's biological clock, so that we know when to sleep and when to wake. The gland detects light reaching it through the eye; when there is no light, it secretes the melatonin into the bloodstream, lowering the body temperature and helping to induce sleep. Melatonin pills contain a synthetic version of the hormone and are commonly used for *jet lag* as well as for *sleep disturbance*. John Nicholls, sales manager of one of America's largest health food shops, claims that sales of the pill have increased dramatically. He explains that it is sold in capsules, tablets, lozenges and mixed with herbs. It is not effective for all insomniacs, but many users have weaned themselves off sleeping tablets as a result of its side effects.

SECTION – 3

Questions 28-40

Questions 28-37

The passage has seven sections labelled A-G.

Which section contains the following information?

Write the correct letter, A-G in boxes 28-35 on your answer sheet.

You may use any letter more than once.

28. the different amounts of sleep that people require

29. an investigation into the results of sleep deprivation

30. some reasons why people may suffer from sleep disorders

31. lifestyle changes which can help overcome sleep-related problems

32. a process by which sleep helps us to remain mentally and physically healthy

33. claims about a commercialised man-made product for sleeplessness

34. the role of physical changes in sleeping habits

35. the processes involved during sleep

Questions 36-40

Do the following statements agree with the information given in the passage?

In boxes, 36-40 on your answer sheet, write

True	*if the statement agrees with the information*
False	*if the statement contradicts the information*
Not Given	*if there is no information on this*

36. Sleep can cure some illnesses.

37. The various stages of sleep occur more than once a night.

38. Dreaming and sleep-walking occur at similar stages of sleep.

39. Sleepers move around a lot during the REM stage of sleep.

40. The body temperature rises relatively early in elderly people.

Reading PracticeTest 3

Answers

1.	Not Given	21.	J
2.	Not Given	22.	K
3.	False	23.	E
4.	Not Given	24.	A
5.	True	25.	G
6.	False	26.	I
7.	False	27.	C
8.	X	28.	A
9.	i	29.	C
10.	v	30.	E
11.	ii	31.	F
12.	ix	32.	B
13.	iv	33.	G
14.	viii	34.	E
15.	False	35.	D
16.	Not Given	36.	Not given
17.	True	37.	True
18.	False	38.	False
19.	True	39.	False
20.	Not given	40.	True

ABSTRACT

WRITING MODULE

This chapter helps the candidates regarding the IELTS General Writing Test Task 1 with its format and strategies for cracking the Writing Task 1. It includes the marking criteria, tips for writing task along with the do's and don't for candidates. It also includes Writing Task 2 with its strategies and skills.

STRATEGIES FOR TASK 1

IELTS WRITING TIPS

THE GENERAL WRITING TEST - TASK 1

The IELTS General Training Writing Test Task 1: The scope of the task is fairly limited, and you can practise extremely similar tasks, which will greatly prepare you for the exam.

The IELTS General Training Task 1 Writing Test

The IELTS General Training Writing Test lasts for 1 hour and includes 2 tasks. Task 1 is a letter and you must write at least 150 words. You should spend about 20 minutes out of the 1 hour for Task 1. Task 2 is an essay and you must write at least 250 words. You should spend about 40 minutes for Task 2.

The Task for the IELTS General Training Task 1 Writing

The IELTS General Training Writing Task 1 asks you to write a letter of a minimum of 150 words in response to some situation or problem. The task will probably ask you to complain about something, to request information, ask for help, to make arrangements and/ or explain a situation. All these are fairly similar tasks.

Marking for the IELTS General Training Task 1 Writing

The IELTS General Training Task 1 Writing will be marked in four areas. You will get a mark from 1 to 9 on Task *Achievement, Coherence & Cohesion, Lexical Resource* and *Grammatical Range* and *Accuracy*. Your final band for Task 1 will be effectively an average of the four marks awarded in these areas. Task 1 writing is less important than Task 2 and to calculate the final writing marks, more weight is assigned to the Task 2 mark than to task 1's mark. To get a good overall marks for The IELTS General Training Writing though, both tasks have to be well answered, so don't hold back on Task 1 or give yourself too little, time to answer it properly.

1. **Task Achievement:** This is where you can really make a difference through careful preparation. This mark grades you on basically "have you answered the question".

It marks whether you have covered all requirements of the task sufficiently and whether you presented, highlighted and illustrated the key points appropriately.

2. **Coherence and Cohesion:** These two are interrelated which is why they are done together. Cohesion is how your writing fits together. Does your writing with its ideas and content flow logically? Coherence is how you are making yourself understood and whether the reader of your writing understands what you are saying. An example of bad coherence and cohesion would be as follows:

1. ***We went to the beach because it was raining.***

Probably, the writer of this sentence does not mean "because" as people don't usually go to the beach when it is raining. The writer should have written:

2. ***We went to the beach although it was raining.***

Sentence 1 has made a cohesion and coherence error (as well as a vocabulary one). "Because" does not join the ideas of the sentence together correctly and, as a result, the reader does not understand what the writer wants to say.

3. **Lexical Resource:** This area looks at the your choice of words. The marker will look at whether the right words are used and whether they are used at the right time in the right place and in the right way. To get a good mark here, the word choice should not only be accurate but wide ranging, natural and sophisticated.

4. **Grammatical Range and Accuracy:** Here the examiner will mark your appropriate, flexible and accurate use of grammatical structures. Many people are worried about their grammar but, as you can see, grammar is only one section of the four used to grade your writing. *IELTS is much more interested in communication rather than grammatical accuracy.* It is, of course, still part of the marking scheme and important as such.

Tips for Writing Task 1

1. Answering the question

Task achievement (answering the question) is one quarter of your total marks and it is an area in which everyone should do well. This is often, however, not the case.

What you must do is to write a letter, which would fully answer the needs of the problem in a real life situation. Even if you have covered all that the question itself asks, have you included everything in the letter needed to realistically perform its function? For example, a question I have seen somewhere gives the candidate the following task:

You have some library books that you are unable to return as a member of your

family in another city has fallen sick and you have had to go and look after him/her.

Write a letter to the library explaining the situation. Apologize for the inconvenience called and say what you are going to do.

You should write at least 150 words.

This seems a fairly typical IELTS General Training Task 1 writing question. Answering the question in a way that will get you a good Task Fulfilment Grade needs a number of things for you to do.

1. Write at least 150 words.

Writing less does not answer the question, which tells you to write at least 150 words. If you write less than 150 words, the examiner marking your paper will give you a maximum of 5 for Task Achievement or even less.

2. Fully do all the things that the question asks you.

In this case, it asks you to do 3 main things:

1. Explain the situation
2. Apologize for the inconvenience
3. Say what you are going to do

The important part is to fully do these things. Don't take one line to explain about your relative – people who do this often don't make the 150 word limit. Enlarge on what the question tells you. Use your imagination. It must be something fairly serious to make you leave town and you must be the only one possible to look after the relative so go into these things. Be realistic as well.

You're writing to a library and you shouldn't make it too personal. Apologizing won't take much space, but you can still devote a couple of sentences to it. Saying what you are going to do should be a full explanation as well.

3. Make your letter realistic to function in a real life situation.

This involves adding other things to the letter, which it may not ask you for, but without which your letter would not perform its function. For this question, it would mean introducing yourself by name, giving your library card membership number, telling the library the titles of the books that you have borrowed, the names of their authors, their library reference numbers, when you borrowed them and when they were due back.

Finally, in this question, the situation might involve you getting a fine for the late books so you could ask politely for that to be cancelled due to the circumstances. Without this information, the letter wouldn't help the library much in real life and, even though the question doesn't ask you specifically to include it, the examiner reading your work will be looking for such things. These are things that are needed to get a 9 for task fulfilment and, theoretically, anyone, whatever their level of English, should be able to get a good mark here.

4. The Opening Greeting of the Letter

Your letter will probably need to be a reasonably *informal letter* to a friend or a *semi-formal letter*. The opening of your letter should reflect which one you are writing.

A friendly letter will open with 'Dear' followed by a name which should then be followed by a comma, eg:

Dear John,

A semi-formal letter will also open with 'Dear' and then be followed by a name, (if you decide that in the situation you would know the name) or by Sir (if it's a man), Madam (if it's a woman) or Sir/Madam, if you don't know, eg:

Dear Mr. Phillips,

Dear Mrs. Phillips,

Dear Sir,

Dear Madam,

Dear Sir/Madam,

The question also might specify how you are to begin, so follow what it says.

5. The Opening Paragraph of the Letter

In a semi-formal letter, I feel it is important to state the reason for the letter straightaway. You could use the following to help you:

I am writing to ask/ tell//inform you that...

I am writing to ask/inquire...

I am writing with regard to...

I am writing with reference to...

I am writing in connection with...

I am writing in response to...

In reply to your letter, I am writing to... (if the question indicates that you have had a letter)

If the letter is a less formal one to a friend, then you should open the letter in a friendlier way. e.g.:

Dear Anil,

Hi there! It's been so long since I've heard from you. I hope you are doing well and I hope all your family are doing fine. I'm pretty good in spite of working hard. Anyway, the reason I'm writing is...

6. The Substance of the Letter

In this section, students have to answer all the above asked questions in the letter. There are some ideas about some words to use in the substance of the letter which will help you to answer the task well.

Asking for Help

I would like you to...

I would be grateful if you could...

I need to ask your advice about...

I'd like to ask for information about...

What I'm looking for is...

Complaining

I'm writing to express my dissatisfaction/annoyance/about...

I'm writing to express my anger at...

I am not happy about...

... is not what I expected/was expecting.

I want to know what you are going to do about this situation.

Thanking

I'm very grateful for...

I'd like to thank you very much for...

I very much appreciated...

Apologizing

I'm very sorry that/about...

Please forgive me for...

I'd like to apologize about...

Please accept my apologies

7. Ending Your Letter

First of all, in English, we often end letters before the sign off with certain phrases. These can be included in most letters and will make your letter seem realistic and polished. For a formal letter, you could use:

If you require any further information, please do not hesitate to contact me. Thanking you in advance for your help, I look forward to hearing from you soon.

For a more informal letter, you could use:

If you need to know anything else, just get in touch with me as soon as you can. Thanks a lot for your help and I hope to hear from you soon.

Be careful, though the IELTS examiners quite rightly look for writing that has been memorised and just repeated, so, if you use expressions like the ones above, make sure that they fit in with the rest of your letter.

Finally, you'll need to sign off your letter. For a formal letter use:

Yours faithfully, OR

Yours sincerely,

Remember, the commas (it makes a good impression on the examiner, if you use good punctuation) and spell, 'sincerely' correctly (a lot of people don't!).

For an informal letter, love is not always appropriate though English speakers use it a lot. It would be better to use:

Regards,

Yours,

Best wishes,

Other Hints for the IELTS General Training Task 1 Writing

1. DON'T copy any part of the question in your answer. This is not your own work and therefore will be disregarded by the examiner and deducted from the word count. You can use individual words but be careful of using 'chunks' of the question text.
2. Don't repeat yourself or the same ideas. This gives a bad impression and the examiner realises that it isn't adding to the content of your letter.
3. If you are weak in English grammar, try to use short sentences. This allows you

to control the grammar and the meaning of your writing much more easily and contributes to a better coherence and cohesion mark. It's much easier to make things clear in a foreign language if you keep your sentences short!

4. Think about the tenses of your verbs. If you're writing about something that happened in the past, your verbs will need to be in the past tense. If you're arranging something in the future, you will need to use the future tense. If it's a habitual action, you'll need the present simple tense and so on. If you have time, a quick check of your verbs at the end of the exam can help you find errors.

5. Don't be irrelevant. Although you can use your imagination to expand on your answer, if any part of your letter is totally unrelated to the question and put in to just put up the word count, then the examiner will not take it into account and deduct it from the word count.

STRATEGIES FOR TASK 2

THE GENERAL WRITING TEST - TASK 2

The IELTS General Training Writing Test

The IELTS General Training Writing Test lasts for 1 hour and includes 2 tasks. Task 1 is a letter and you must write at least 150 words. You should spend about 20 minutes out of 1 hour for Task 1. Task 2 is an essay and you must write at least 250 words. You should spend about 40 minutes for Task 2.

The Task for the IELTS General Training Task 2 Writing

1. Short Essay for Minimum 250 words

The IELTS General Training Writing Task 2 asks you to write a short essay of a minimum of 250 words. The essay is usually a discussion of a subject of general interest. You may have to present and justify your opinion about something, give the solution to a problem or compare differing ideas or viewpoints.

2. Marking for the IELTS General Training Task 2 Writing

Your task will be marked in four areas. You will get a mark from 1 to 9 on Task response, Coherence and Cohesion, Lexical Resource and Grammatical Range and Accuracy. Your final band for Task 2 will be effectively an average of the four marks awarded in these areas. Task 2 writing is more important than Task 1 and to calculate the final writing mark, more weight is assigned to the Task 2 mark than to the Task 1's mark. To get a good overall mark though, both tasks have to be well answered, so don't hold back on Task 1 or give yourself too little time to answer it properly.

(a) Task Response

This mark grades you on the content of your essay. It marks whether you have fully addressed all parts of the task. The examiner wants you in your essay to have a fully developed answer to the question given with relevent and extended ideas and support. The support is the facts that you use to back up your ideas. Support is very important in Task 2. You need to bring in facts from your own experience in order to support your ideas.

3. Paragraphing for the IELTS General Training Task 2 Writing

Very often the examiner has to face with a 'sea' of writing with no breaks from start to finish. The best writings are those where there are paragraphs separated by an empty line and also indented. In this way, your ideas are separated clearly. It shows and gives organization to your writing and makes it more readable.

For Task 2, have a paragraph break after your introduction, and then for every differing section of your separate ideas with the supporting evidence. Then have a final paragraph for your conclusion. You should aim to have 3 or 4 paragraphs plus the introduction and conclusion.

4. Ideas to Think about for the IELTS General Training Task 2 Writing

(a) Timing: The exam paper recommends that you spend about 40 minutes on this question and this is about right. Remember that Task 2 gives more to your final writing band and so you should make sure that you have enough time after Task 1 to properly answer Task 2. Some students do Task 2 first in order to make sure that Task 2 is answered well before they get onto Task 1. There is no problem with this but make sure, you write the 150 words to give a good answer for Task 1 as well.

So, whatever you decide to do about your approach to Task 1 and Task 2 in the writing paper, make sure that you spend approximately 20 minutes on Task 1 and 40 minutes on Task 2. This should give you the right amount of time to provide good answers to both the tasks.

(b) Answering the question: First of all, read the question very carefully in order to see exactly what it asks you. Very often, there will be more than 1 part to the question; sometimes even 3 or 4 parts. When you produce your answer, you must answer all the different parts of the question. How much you produce on each part depends on how important you think it is.

(c) Planning: Just take a scrap of paper and jot down some ideas that you are going to use in your essay. Then you can divide the ideas into 3 or 4 paragraphs in a logical order. This shouldn't take you long and the structure that this will give your essay will be well worth the time that you spend doing it.

Format for Writing the Essay

1. Introduction

Your introduction should first say what you understand by the question. Then give the main issue or issues that you intend to bring into your answer. Don't go into any detail; you can save that for the later paragraphs.

Finally, the question often asks you to take up a position over an issue. There is no right answer for putting your views in the beginning and then explaining this through out the essay, or developing your opinion through your essay and stating your final stance at the end. I personally like the opinion at the start of the essay. Quickly and clearly, answer the question, making your attitude plain. Don't give any reasons. Again, that's what the body of your essay is for. You don't have to do it this way though. You can wait until your conclusion to give your position as regards the question.

2. The Body of Your Essay

You should aim to have 3 or 4 paragraphs in your answer. This is not exact. You can write more or fewer paragraphs, as your answer requires. Remember, you've only got about 40 minutes to cover all the question areas, so don't be too ambitious and try to write too much.

In the body of your essay, you should do several things. You need to examine all the parts of the question. Remember, there is often more than 1 question contained in the essay question text. You need to look at all that is asked and look at both sides of every issue. The IELTS essay questions usually ask you something which has two or more points of view, and you need to consider both sides of every argument no matter what your opinion is.

Look below at the example. The question asks whether or not you believe, whether societies should use capital punishment. There are, of course, two points of view:

1. capital punishment should be used and
2. capital punishment shouldn't be used.

Let's say for example that you don't believe that capital punishment should be used by societies. No matter what point of view you have, you should look at both sides, though naturally, your writing will favour the position that you have taken. Give the reasons why you don't believe in capital punishment, but then look at the opposing view and say why you don't accept it. In this way, you will show the reader your powers of analysis when looking at such an issue.

Don't forget that when you have finished looking at this issue, there is a second part of the question to be analysed too.

As we said earlier, your ideas need to be supported by examples and it is in the body of your essay that they should appear. For every idea that you present, try and give an example from your own experience that shows that your idea is right.

An example from your own experience means something that you know from your life, from your country's news or history or anything that you have read anywhere. You can actually invent examples if you need as long as they seem realistic and believable. The examiner is probably not going to research anything you write about.

The example below should illustrate what we have been discussing here.

3. Conclusion

Simply review the main points (being careful not to restate them exactly or repeat all your examples) and briefly describe your feelings about the topic; this provides an answer to all parts of the question. An anecdote can also end your essay in a useful way.

An Example of the IELTS General Training Task 2 Writing

Here is a possible question that would be typical for a Task 2 essay question.

"Do you believe that societies ought to enforce capital punishment or are there alternative forms of punishment that would be better used?"

First of all, you need to consider the question. What does it ask? Straightaway, you can see that it asks 2 things.

It wants to know if you believe that the society should use capital punishment (cp) and it also wants to know if you can offer any alternatives to the capital punishment. Your answer should give a balanced view of both the parts of this question. What is important to realize is that there is no correct answer here. You can present any point of view as long as you can support it.

So, in your planning stage, you should have a roadmap for the introduction, each paragraph and the conclusion. Here is my brief plan for the essay.

Introduction

- ★ What Capital Punishment or CP? Where is it used? Differing opinions.
- ★ I don't believe in Capital Punishment.
- ★ There are alternative punishments.

Body

1. Inhumane - we shouldn't sink to the level of criminals.
2. We can get convictions wrong; prisoners can be released if there's an error or they are mentally ill. Examples.
3. Alternative punishments: Life means life; hospitals for criminally insane. Costs more but society has a duty to care.
4. Many countries favour it and they say it works. Prisons are too full. Killers deserve nothing less. Some crimes deserve it. Not my morals though.

Conclusion

I don't agree. We can do other things. Avoid mistakes and make the modern society a humane one.

The above is a basic plan of how I want to write my essay. It's not rigid. I can change my ideas and format as I write if I feel I can do better.

So, below is an example essay using the plan above as a basis.

Example Essay for the IELTS General Training Task 2 Writing

Capital Punishment (CP) is the killing of a criminal for a crime that he has committed. Previously most countries employed this method of punishment but nowadays, it is much less widely used. I personally do not believe that societies today should use capital punishment and I also believe that there are alternative punishments that can be used.

My main argument against capital punishment is that I believe we do not have the right to kill another human being regardless of the crime. I don't believe in the old religious maxim of 'an eye for an eye.' Modern societies shouldn't turn to such barbaric punishments.

Another argument against capital punishment is that people can be wrongly convicted and executed. If a man is in prison, he can be released if later proved not guilty. If he is dead, there is nothing that can be done. In the UK, a group of supposed terrorists were convicted of murder in Birmingham in the 1970s. They were proved innocent about 15 years later and released. If they had been executed, innocent people would have died.

There are alternative punishments available. For severe crimes life imprisonment can be given with criminals imprisoned for the rest of their lives. Also a lot of horrific crimes are committed by people who are mentally sick. These people are not responsible for their actions and can be kept safely and permanently in secure hospitals. Yes, this costs a lot more but I believe it is the duty of the society to do this.

There are arguments for Capital Punishment(CP). Many people feel its threat stops serious crimes and that criminals deserve nothing less. It's cheaper and keeps the prisons manageable. I can understand this point of view but I cannot agree with it.

So, in conclusion, I don't believe in capital punishment, as there are less barbaric alternatives available. We can avoid horrific mistakes and make the modern society a humane one.

WRITING TEST 1

TASK 1

Bad experience with a cruise

You have taken a cruise and have been disappointed with the experience. Write a letter to the cruise provider and specify.

- ★ what went wrong?
- ★ how did you feel about it?
- ★ what do you want to be done about it?

Dear Sir/Madam,

My name is Ankush and I am writing to bring your attention to an unsatisfactory experience we had with the Christmas Cruises on December 25, 2010.

First, contrary to what was in the advertisement, the boat was old and homely. It was cold inside from the beginning, but when a hundred passengers boarded, the windows became misted due to poor ventilation, which made it impossible to enjoy the views of the harbour.

Second, even though we were provided with a 'private table', there were so many private tables that we were literally sitting elbow to elbow with other passengers. The cheap, unsteady tables were put so close to each other that we became barricaded and had to ask other people to stand up and let us pass to get the food or to use the washroom. This all provided us with the feeling of growing embarrassment incompatible with enjoying the cruise and the Christmas spirit.

In these circumstances, we do not feel that it is unreasonable to expect a full refund of the money paid to you following the misrepresentation of what Christmas Cruises were offering. We expect, therefore, a refund of the full amount.

Yours faithfully,

Ankush

TASK 2

You should spend about 40 minutes on this task.

Today, the high sales of popular consumer goods reflect the power of advertising and not the real needs of the society in which they are sold. To what extent do you agree or disagree?

You should write at least 250 words.

Nowadays, millions of companies produce billions of products and the role of advertising is quite obvious. Ads help consumers to find the goods or services of their needs. However, do our needs grow equally fast as the number of products? Some market analysts insist modern commercials are not merely matchmakers of a product and a consumer, but actively interfere with the buyer's desires, developing artificial needs.

Undoubtedly, advertisement guides people through the market, and serves those who do not have time to learn the differences between goods. These products are probably the same, but loyalty to a particular brand, formed by a commercial helps make a choice. When a person buys one mobile phone out of 50 models, he thinks he made his choice himself. But that was a commercial who told him about the features of this phone.

Nevertheless, ads not only inform us about new goods, but force people to want them. This can be even useful, for example, for someone who suffers from back pains and without commercials, he would never imagine there are new mattresses which could ease his/her pains.

Unfortunately, promoters now operate our minds more aggressively. Commercials no longer promote products, but lifestyles. They tell us to purchase things just because they are fashionable or up to date with the image of a successful person. And we buy new cars, gadgets and clothes in order to match this image and not because old ones are no longer usable.

Personally, I think that high sales of popular commodities are the result of new promotional technologies. The best illustration of that is that everyone now is concerned mostly about how a new mobile phone will reflect his/her personality, a new shirt – his/her image, or will a new car make his/her colleagues feel jealous?

WRITING TEST 2

TASK 1

You recently had your computer fixed at the local computer store. However you are not pleased with the service you received.

Write a letter to the store manager. In the letter

- ✭ describe the situation.
- ✭ explain why you are dissatisfied.
- ✭ say what you want the manager to do.

Write at least 150 words.

You do NOT need to write your own address.

Begin your letter as follows: Dear Sir or Madam,

Dear Sir or Madam,

I am writing to express my dissatisfaction with the service I received at your establishment.

Actually, the computer I have bought at your store on the late January was quite good. However, after just half a year things got wrong. Some programs were getting frozen frequently. When I took my computer to your specialist and tried to explain the problem to the technician Aniket, he refused to take my computer into service because the problem did not appear that time. I was trying to convince him to spend more time to identify the reason it is getting stuck, but he was rude and impatient explaining this is the end of his shift. On the next day, another technician listened to me carefully and fixed my computer in 10 minutes.

I suppose your employee, Aniket is not suitable for his position because of his unprofessionalism. I suggest you to employ someone more skilled and with better personality in order not to cause your customers to lose their time like me.

Yours faithfully,

Rakesh Sharma

TASK 2

You should spend about 40 minutes on this task.

Some people believe that children's leisure activities must be educational, otherwise, they are a complete waste of time.

Do you agree or disagree?

Give reasons for your answer and include any relevant examples from your experience.

You should write at least 250 words.

These days children spend so much time at school and attend various additional classes that this makes some educational specialists feel pity for them. They suggest giving kids more spare time to play and have fun. Meanwhile, there is an opinion that youngsters should do only those activities that benefit their knowledge and educate them, and I totally agree with this point of view.

Of course, the volume of the information children receive at school and ought to memorize is enormous and they should be given some free time to relax. Playing with others is essential to develop communication skills and this also gives the young brains some rest.

Although, we have to admit that in our competitive world, the more time a kid devotes to the study process, the better life he can achieve. There are ways to make playing with others very educational and parents should encourage their children to play games which make the brain work. For example, kids could have a competition combining physical activity and some kind of trivia on geography, like we had in our childhood. Moreover, even computer games can be very intelligent. There are so many electronic entertainments which teach languages, give information on history and geography that children addicted to computers could become very smart and educated.

In addition, unattended kids hardly makes proper use of their leisure time. If it happens, children just watch TV or get under peer pressure. They, unfortunately do not have skills of analyzing and filtering what is bad or what is good. Education through games, instead makes them occupied and at the same time teaches how to analyze.

To conclude with, education through fun is not very exhausting for kids, but its usefulness can be great. It would be a shame to devote this time to TV or other entertainment.

WRITING TEST 3

TASK 1

You are employed full-time and also doing a part-time evening course. You are not able to continue the course.

Write a letter to the course lecturer. In the letter,

- ✯ explain why you cannot continue the course.
- ✯ describe the situation.
- ✯ say what you will be doing.

Write at least 150 words.

You do NOT need to write your own address.

Begin your letter as follows: Dear ....,

Dear Dr. Ahuja,

I am writing to inform you that I no longer have a possibility to attend your evening lectures on treating emergencies.

As I told you earlier, I received a position of a nurse at the Family Hospital. My shift ends at 5 pm and since I have got a lot of overtime job recently, I find myself unable to be on time at your lectures, which begin at 5.30 pm. This disappoints me a lot, since I value and respect your course and your experience.

I would be grateful if you could consider letting me to study your course myself. As of my job is closely related to the treatment of the injured, I feel I am able to learn myself every point of the course in practice. In addition, I have already read almost every book you recommended as the supplementary reading for your lectures.

I hope to get your approval on this matter soon. I am looking forward to receiving your response.

yours sincerely,

Ankit

TASK 2

You should spend about 40 minutes on this task.

It has been proved that smoking kills. In some countries, it has been made illegal for people to smoke in all public places except in certain areas. All countries should make these rules.

Do you agree or disagree with this statement?

You should write at least 250 words.

The idea of banning smoking from public places always was a very controversial one. Those who defend smoking on streets and in offices refer to human rights and the fact that tobacco is legal. Others hold an opinion that since there are undeniable proofs that cigarettes cause lethal diseases not only to smokers but to the surrounding people, smoking should be allowed only in special places. I totally agree with the idea of making smoking legal in certain places only.

On one hand, it is the society who makes smokers to smoke and it would be not fair just to put them into exile and consider the problem solved. Since we sell them tobacco, they should have the right to use it wherever they want.

On the other hand, those who do not smoke should have the right to breathe clean air. When somebody is smoking cigarette, health of the non-smokers is under attack. Personally, I am a former smoker, but even for me, breathing tobacco smell is unbearable. It not only makes people temporarily feel bad, but also causes long-term effects. There are researches showing that the so called 'passive smoking' could be even worse for health than smoking itself. Causing damage to anyone's health is illegal, and that is why there is no excuse for smoking in public places.

Another reason for this is the fact that not every legal action is allowed in public. Moral, cultural and judicial limitations do exist. For example, there are toilets for people's bladder and nobody is allowed to urinate on streets. Tobacco is much more dangerous than that so there is no doubt every country should consider moving smokers to special places.

To conclude with, every country must think of the well-being of its citizens and take steps to protect them from the dangerous effects of tobacco by banning smoking from public places.

ABSTRACT

SPEAKING MODULE

The IELTS speaking has three parts Part 1, II & III which iuncludes Interview Sessions, Cue Cards & Followup Querries. We endavour to help the candidates with the collection of the most popular 50 questions for part I and the most popular Cue Cards of the IELTS exam along with the followup queries.

Chapter 5 : Speaking Strategies, Skills and Guidelines

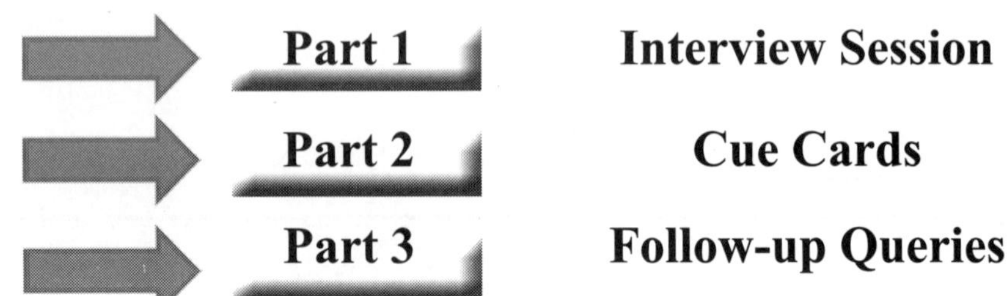

Paper Duration: 15 To 20 Minutes

Phase A: Home/Study/Work

Phase B: Likes & Dislikes

Food/Shopping/Festivals/Markets/Books /Sports, etc.

SAMPLE QUESTIONS FOR PHASE A (WARM UP QUERIES)

Home/Study/Work

- DO you work, or are you a student ?
- Can you tell me something about your studies?
- What is your favourite subject?
- What is your study plan ?

SAMPLE QUESTIONS FOR PHASE - B

What do you eat for breakfast?

STRATEGY NO. 1: BE CULTURAL APPROPRIATELY

For example: While answering this question, make sure that certain diet/breakfast must belong to the culture of your state.

Will people's diet change in future?

STRATEGY NO. 2: BE VERSATILE IN ANSWERING

For example: Do discuss some other cuisines apart from your state.

Here the examiner wants to see your exposure.

Do you have any hobbies?

STRATEGY NO. 3: UPDATE ANSWER

It is necessary to be up-to-date in answering the questions. Don't follow rote memorization. Whatever present hobbies, the candidate is adhered to answer only opt for that.

What are the most popular sports in your country?

STRATEGY NO. 4: ALWAYS USE CURRENT UPDATES

For example: While answering this question, make sure that whatever is going on currently should be discussed.Try to use your IQ level.

How do you spend your spare time?

STRATEGY NO. 5: BE PRACTICAL IN ANSWERING

For example: Do the examiner come to know what exactly your way and standard of living. Never try to be overconfident in answering.

What kind of musical instrument do you enjoy in playing? Do you play a musical instrument?

STRATEGY NO. 6: BE OPTIMISTIC IN YOUR APPROACH AND TRY TO COVER THE ANSWERS IN INTRODUCTORY LINES

Sometimes, Questions are beyond one's comprehension, so don't lose heart. Try to introduce the subject of the Question For example, Playing an instrument is not the cup of every one's tea. While answering, follow an optimistic approach and say presently, "I don't know but I really wish to learn flute/piano, etc." or Use some introductory lines for music, for example: "Music is the food for the soul", etc.

CUE-CARD 1

DESCRIBE YOUR FAVOURITE MOVIE

You should say:

Which the movie is it

Why has the movie impressed you so much?

You can give your own suggestions.

And Explain how it influenced you.

Which is the movie?

- *Slum Dog Millionaire*
- *Winner of Oscar award*

Why has the movie impressed you so much?

- *Throws light on the life of people living in slums.*
- *Talent also resides in slums.*

SLUM DOG

You can give your own suggestion.

- *Try to direct these kinds of movies in INDIA.*
- *Adopt some different title because it hurts the dignity of INDIA.*

And explain how it influences you.

- *The theme of the film really enhances the dignity of humanity residing in slums.*
- *It changes the outlook of the people.*

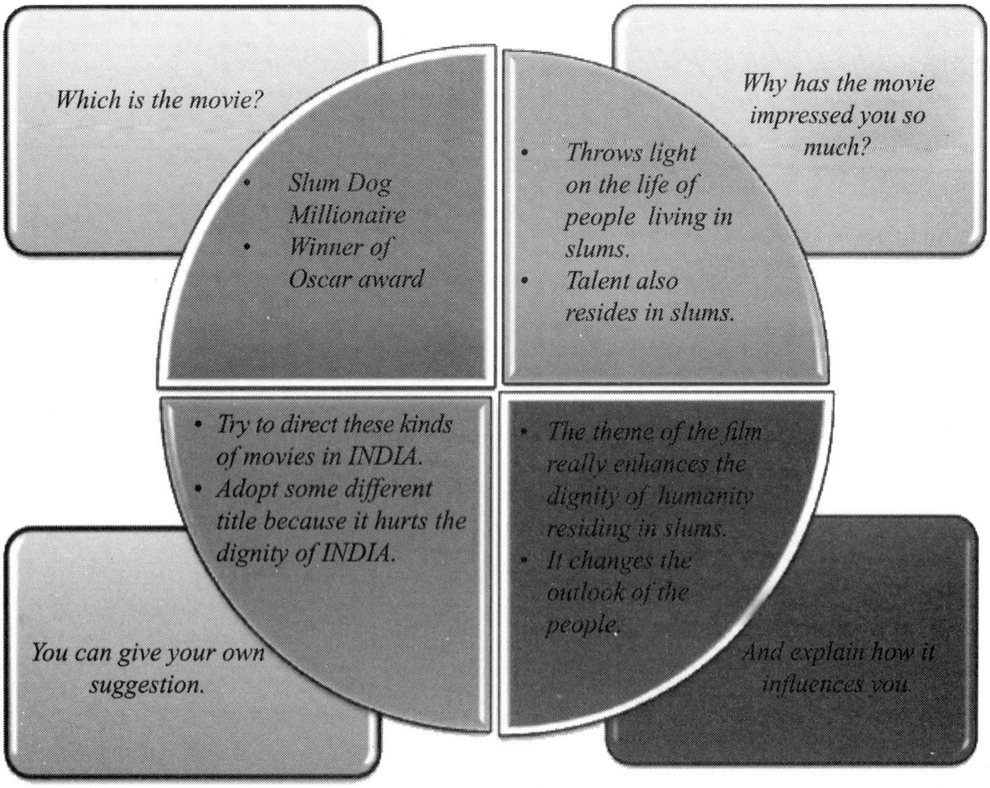

SUMMARIZATION: 'JOURNEY FROM RAGS TO RICHES'

STRATEGY NO. 7: TO CRACK CUE-CARDS

STEP NO. 1 : MAKE A GRID: When the examiner offers 2 minutes to think over the topic, make a Grid, and decide the title of the Q- Card.

STEP NO. 2 : ANSWER THE QUERIES: Make the notes and answers of all the following questions of the CUE-CARD.

STEP NO. 3 : SYNCHRONIZE THE NOTES WITH SUMMARIZATION: Now start speaking by using the pronouns like It, This, I, etc. You can use three types of pronouns like the *First Person, Second Person, Third Person*, etc.

CUE-CARD 2

DESCRIBE YOUR FAVOURITE GADGET

You should say:

Which is the gadget

Why you like that gadget?

How does it helps you?

And explain, whether it brings change in to your life.

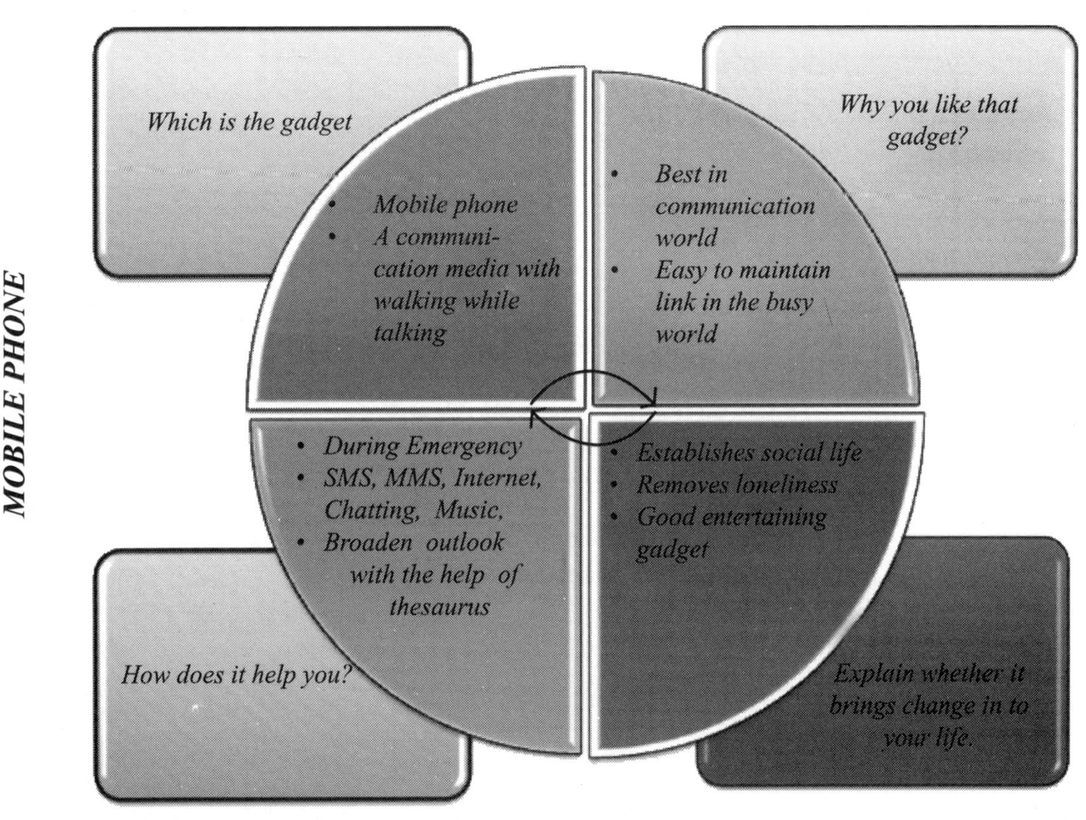

SUMMARIZATION: "without this gadget life is handicap"

CUE-CARD 3

DESCRIBE ANY NATIONAL DAY

You should say:

Which is the day?

Why is it celebrated?

How is it celebrated?

And explain, what you do on this day?

STRATEGIES TO APPROACH THE CUE-CARDS

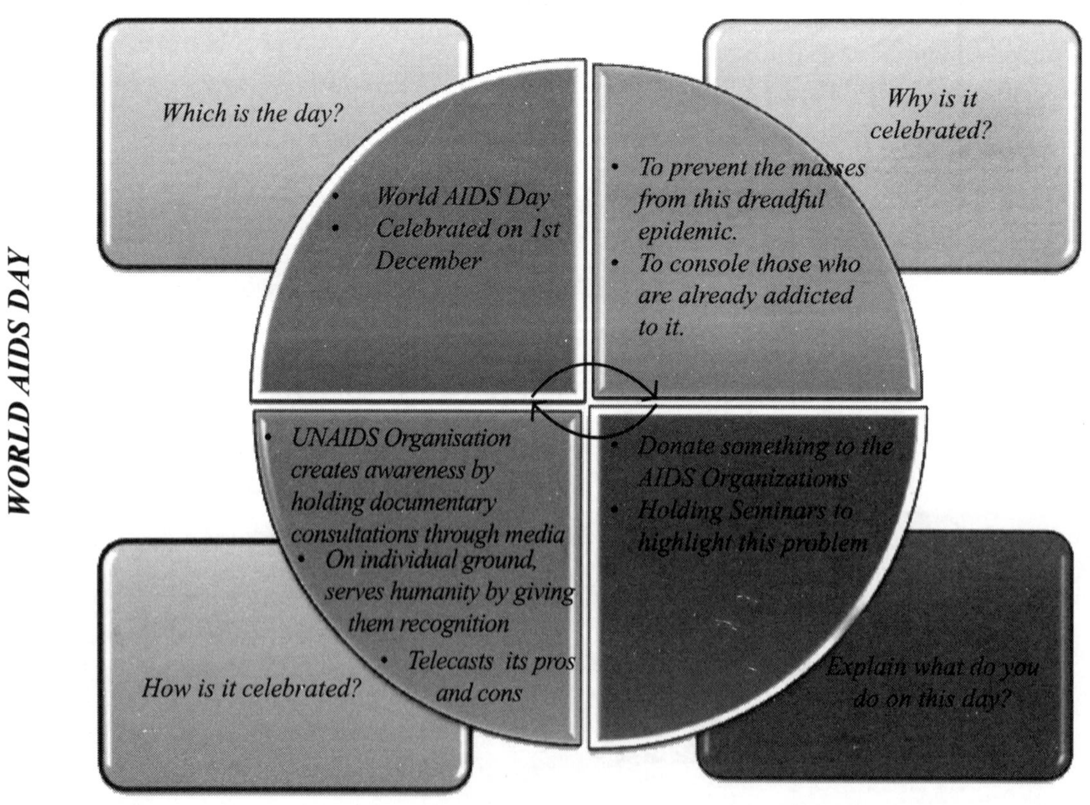

SUMMARIZATION: 'JOURNEY FROM HEAVEN TO HELL'

PART 3

FOLLOW-UP QUESTIONS

1. ***If the Cue-Cards are related to the ideal teacher then in Part 3 follow on concept will be applied, i.e., all the questions are related to education, school and college.***

JUST FOLLOW THIS EXAMPLE

- ★ What is the importance of a teacher in our lives?
- ★ Should a teacher be versatile?
- ★ Do you think teachers should update their knowledge?

2. ***If the Cue-Cards are related to technology in Part 3, the follow on concept will be applied, i.e., all the questions are related to science, communication and inventions.***

JUST FOLLOW THIS EXAMPLE

- ★ What are the important inventions of the century?
- ★ What are the destructive uses of technology?
- ★ Which forms of technology are you using at home/office?
- ★ What is the future of technology?

3. ***If the Cue-Cards are related to shopping, then in Part 3 the follow on Concept will be applied, i.e., all the questions are related to youngsters, males and females both.***

JUST FOLLOW THIS EXAMPLE

- ★ Do you like shopping?
- ★ Do you think window-shopping is wastage of time?
- ★ What are the benefits and drawbacks of consumerism?
- ★ What are the advantages and disadvantages of credit cards?

GUIDELINES FOR SPEAKING MODULE

DAY Of INTERVIEW

SUCCESSFUL TIPS FOR STUDENTS

- **BE LOUD & CLEAR**
- **MAINTAIN THE RATE OF SPEECH**
- **TAKE A DEEP BREATH & RELAX**
- **STRICT TO INTERVIEW ETIQUETTES**
- **POSITIVE BODY LANGUAGE/DRESS PROPERLY**

COMMON ERRORS

BEING EXCESSIVELY POLITE

Explanation: Foreign Examiners can become uncomfortable when the candidate is overly respectful.

Example of Error: Saying sir or maam, and waiting to be asked to sit down on the chair for the candidate.

How to Avoid this Error: Be polite and respectful, but not excessively so. Say, 'Hi' instead of 'Good morning sir/maam.'

THINKING THAT THE IELTS EXAMINER IS A STRANGER TO YOUR COUNTRY

Explanation: The IELTS examiner almost certainly lives in the same country as you and has done so for some time.

Example of Error: Saying things such as 'Welcome to the my country!'

How to Avoid this Error: Showing that you know that the examiner is familiar with your country by saying, 'In my country as I am sure that you are aware...'

NOT SPEAKING LIKE AN INDIVIDUAL

Explanation: Although it is common to think as being in part of a group for many people, most IELTS examiners come from backgrounds where they expect and prefer individuals to give their own personal answers to questions.

Example of Error: For example, answering a question by saying, 'Of course I am from ...., so I like.......'

How to Avoid this Error: When giving your own opinion say: "In my personal opinion....

USING STEREOTYPES

Explanation: Describing one ethnic or national group as unique and deserving, special treatment is offensive to many people.

Example of Error: For example, answering a question by saying, "---- people are the most hospitable people in the world."

How to Avoid this Error: Recognizing that there are many different types of people in the world and that no one country or ethnic group can be the best at anything. So saying something such as the following would be acceptable:

"My people have a reputation for being very hospitable..."

TRYING TO BEFRIEND THE EXAMINER

Explanation: Trying to find out information about the examiner such as "So your name is..?" or "Where are you from?"

Example of Error: Be polite and smile only.

How to Avoid this Error: Remember that you are taking part in a test, not a social activity.

DRESSING INAPPROPRIATELY

Explanation: The IELTS speaking exam is a formal exam. You should dress formally and thereby gain the respect of the Examiner.

Example of Error: Wearing casual clothes.

How to Avoid this Error: Dress like you were going to a job interview.

TRYING TO MAKE PHYSICAL CONTACT WITH THE IELTS EXAMINER

Explanation: This is usually through trying to shake hands with the Examiner. It is a formal exam, so physical contact between the Candidate and the Examiner is inappropriate and may the Examiner feel uncomfortable.

Example of Error: Trying to shake hand with the Examiner.

How to Avoid this Error: Avoid it unless the examiner chooses to shake your hand. Then you probably should do so, so as to avoid being disrespectful to the IELTS Examiner..

INTRUDING ON THE EXAMINER'S PERSONAL SPACE.

Explanation: Most Examiners are from countries where it is important to respect people's personal space; which is around a handshake distance from another person (30 cm). Many people, especially native English speaking Examiners, frequently feel uncomfortable and offended when strangers intrude into their area of personal space.

Example of Error: Leaning across the interview table into the examiner.

DO'S AND DON'T'S FOR IELTS SPEAKING EXAM

DO'S FOR IELTS

- ✭ Give extented responses.
- ✭ The IELTS instructor gives more weightage to comprehensive and complete answers.
- ✭ Be concise and to the point.
- ✭ Don't beat about the bush in front of the IELTS examiner.
- ✭ Be grammatically correct.
- ✭ Try to use correct tenses and connectors.
- ✭ Speak in simple, small sentences.
- ✭ Usage of appropriate English words.
- ✭ Don't use slang language like wanna, gonna, etc.
- ✭ Usage of proverbs, phrases, idioms and metaphors.
- ✭ Be a Trouble-shooter.
- ✭ If the question is not clear Avoid controversies use words like sorry/pardon.
- ✭ Speak in a nice and pleasant tone.
- ✭ Use synonyms by substituting meanings.

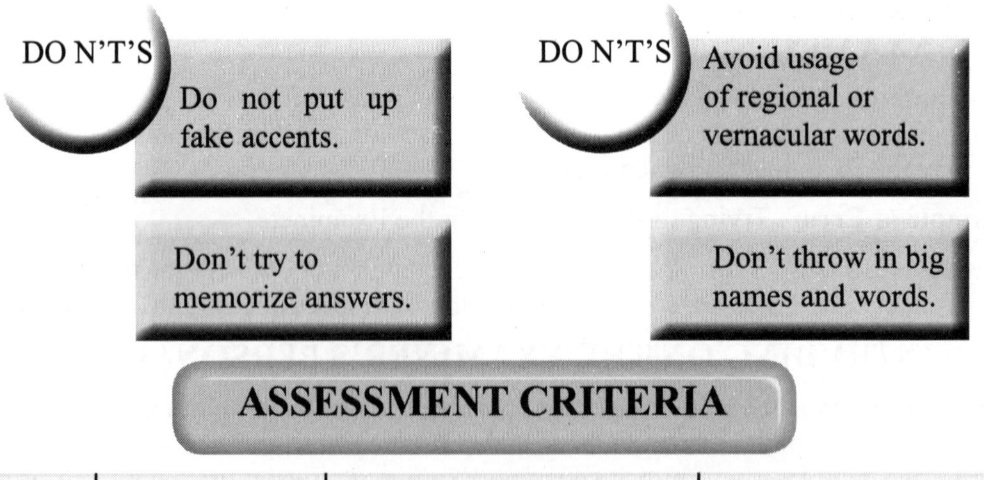

MOST POPULAR 50 QUESTIONS (INTERVIEW SESSION)

1. **What is your full name ? What should I call you?**

Ans. My name is …… Ankit Bhardwaj. You can call me ANKIT.

2. **Can I see your ID?**

Ans. Sure …. Please.

FAMILY

3. **Tell me something about your family?**

Ans. Well….. I belong to a simple, small and nuclear family. I am living with adorable parents and two small sisters. All coordinate with one another and live happily. I must say God has blessed me 'A CLOSE KNIT FAMILY'.

4. **What do you like doing most with your family?**

Ans. I like to have long meals, amusement, fun and frolic, would like to tease my sisters, sharing griefs and sorrows with them. It is a common saying – 'The family which eats together, lives together and laughs together is truly a close knit family.'

5. **Who are close to you in your family?**

Ans. Well… I am very close to my mother, 'A true picture of maternity'. She cooks what I want to eat. She loves and teaches me what is good or bad for me. She is really a very virtuous lady with the blend of passionate feelings of a child. I wish to salute this real role model and admire this wonderful creation of God on this planet!

6. **In what way is your family important to you?**

Ans. My family is everything to me. My family members are my best friends and they support me in every real challenge of my life. I know they are always with me, no matter what. They are not only my best friends but we truly are tied with strong bonds of respect, unity and strength. *That's why I say my family is my real earned wealth and strength.*

WORK

7. **Do you work or are you a student?**

Ans. I am a hardworking person. Presently, I am doing both the tasks simultaneously. In morning hours, I usually go for my orientation classes of language as I am fond of learning linguistics and in the afternoon, I am working as an executive in a reputed company.

8. What are your responsibilities at work ?

Ans. To keep an eye upon the junior executives for maintaining organisational goals and objectives. So keeping supervision over them, checking their targets as well as maintaining coordination and proper communication are my primary jobs. Thorough commitment to work is my first and last responsibility towards work.

STUDY

9. Do you work, or are you a student?

Ans. I am a student at the moment. I am studying English Linguistics and literature together and hoping to get more and more excel in this field.

10. Why do you choose this course or job?

Ans. Honestly speaking, as everyone knows English is a global language. It serves both socially as well as professionally. Because what I believe socially it is the order of the day and professionally it is "A Bag of Handsome Perks & Incentives."

11. What is the most difficult thing about your studies or job?

Ans. The most difficult thing about my studies is its grammatical rules and of course, the lexical part. It's really hard to remember the high profile words and proverbs. Moreover, grammatical rules limit my tendency to learn the things.

12. What type of study most of the students prefer these days?

Ans. Very interesting question, see…… The ultimate goal of every education is to earn well.So most of the students these days tend to fall upon more professional studies despite of academic ones. As these type of vocational studies widen up their empirical outlook and open their arenas for the professional world.

HOBBIES

13. What are your hobbies?

Ans. There is no one thing I'm obsessed about. I have various interests. I am a keen cook and love to make new dishes. I love reading books. I am creative too and love to follow new musical tracks every day. Frankly speaking, hobbies add charms to life and pull out the hidden talents and abilities.

14. What do you like about your hobbies?

Ans. Well….the thing that really fascinates me about my hobbies are that it pulls out my hidden talents and abilities. It brings out a positive change in my life. It proves to be a creative utilisation of time. It is the best way to refuel my body and mind.

15. What type of hobbies are popular among teenagers in your country?

Ans. Actually, hobbies are personal tastes of every individual. As far as my country, teenage hobbies are concerned, I must say among boys like to getting involved into Online Friends, Regular Visitor of Orkut, Facebook and Twitter, Net surfing, Visiting Health Resorts, Gyms and Spa, sending SMS, etc. and among Girls are Reading, Story books, Solving, Puzzles, Chatting, Tidbits, Creative Arts, Music, Sports, etc.

FREE TIME, LEISURE

16. What are the best ways to utilise your free time?

Ans. 'Hobby a day keeps the doldrums away.' So the best way to utilise your free time is to get completely involved in doing what you like the most. It is really beneficial for everyone to cultivate a suitable hobby to help in the proper channelization of free time.

17. Do people have more free time now than in the past?

Ans. It's really quite ironical to say, as we are living in the gadgetry and luxurious world where labour saving machines, such as washing machines and dishwashers are prevailing but still people are too busy in the rat race of earning and spending money. They don't have time to spend with their relations. But in the past, all work was manually handled yet people had time to eat and laugh together.

18. What is the impact of leisure activities on the society?

Ans. The impact of leisure activities on the society is spectacular. It becomes a pattern or style of living for the entire society. Everyone follows the same pattern of living and they coordinate their lives accordingly. They can plan their schedules and programmes as per each other's conveniences.

FRIEND, FRIENDSHIP

19. How do you usually contact your friends?

Ans. Well… I usually get very less time to contact my friends but I always try my every level best to call them or chat with them online.

20. Are friends as important to you as your family?

Ans. Friends and family both are invaluable and no doubt, both act as a four-leaf clover, 'hard to find and lucky to have'...

21. Do you think friendships change as we get older?

Ans. Very true: Gone are those days when friends were truly loved forever, nowadays fake friendships are in the air via following technological advancements like the Facebook or Twitter. Nobody remembers his/her childhood friends.

22. Whom do you call a best friend?

Ans. According to my opinion, a Best Friend is much beyond roaming together and sharing good moments. It is about a long lasting friendship with someone and coming to rescue of a person from the worst phase of life. Friendship with your best friend is eternal.

HOME TOWN

23. Describe your hometown. (Individual Opinion, because candidate has to answer according to the place where he/she is residing.)

24. Is your hometown in the grip of problems?

Ans. Undoubtedly, the general problems of my city these days are overpopulated streets, pollution, traffic embezzlements, etc. Some problems shiver down my spine like the evils of female foeticide and hooliganism.

25. What changes would you like to have in your hometown?

Ans. Very interesting question. Well if I have been given an opportunity to change my hometown, my first priority will be to provide homes to the slums, then encourage each and every student of the city to be literate and educated and last but not the least is to bring technical back up for my city.

TRAVEL

26. Do you think it is true that travel broadens the mind?

Ans. I do, yes…it is true. Travel and change of place impart new vigour to the mind. Travellers never think that they are foreigners. Rather, you see different ways of living, eating, drinking, interacting with others and it allows you to see your own culture more objectively.

27. Do young people and older people get benefits from travelling?

Ans. Well ……for youngsters travelling is an adventurous experience but, for the older people, it is more of relaxation than enjoyment because while travelling, they get switched off from their regular duties and routine work. Moreover, it is advantageous for both the generations to go for travelling as it is an eye opener when we observe people of different states or countries and are familiarized with their lifestyles. It's common saying – 'The World is a Book, and those who do not travel read only a page.'

28. How do you usually travel to work or college?

Ans. Well…… the means of transport is the best source of travelling from one place to another. Generally, I travel to place of my work via Metro as it is the cheapest means of transport as well as faster and petrol savvy.

29. What place do you like to visit most?

Ans. My country, India is a tourist's paradise. Well…if I get an opportunity to visit some place, then I would like to see Kashmir, the real paradise on earth. It is a complete blend of natural beauty, ethnic splendour and cultural diversity. It is the 'CROWN HEAD' of India.

ENGLISH LANGUAGE/LANGUAGE LEARNING

30. How do the people in your country feel about English being the world language?

Ans. There is no such feeling in learning the English language. Everyone knows it is a global language, so learning it is automatically inevitable and everyone has to embrace this global lingua franca not only for communication but also for their economic benefits.

31. Do you think the culture of English Speaking Countries as well as the English language dominate the whole world?

Ans. Undoubtedly… I do believe that the usage of Internet really allows the scope of English on international grounds. It becomes a trendy language these days. No doubt, these days it has become the wine upon the lips.

32. When and where you began studying English? Do you face any problem while studying English?

Ans. As you know, I belong to India so English is not my mother tongue… Being not my native language, I began learning this language in my school when I was 5 years old. Learning the English language for the first time can be difficult. However, when done in an exciting and humourous way, learning English vocabulary and grammar are less confusing and more enjoyable.

33. What is the most effective way of learning English?

Ans. The best way of learning English is to listen properly. It can be with any source like English Native Speakers, Some English Audio DVD's or CD's, Watching English Movies, etc.

FESTIVAL

34. What is the most important festival of your country?

Ans. AHHHH…. A festival of lights, i.e., Diwali is the most important festival of my country. It comes in the month of October or November. It is related to the Hindu and Sikh history. It brings everyone together under the roof of happiness and prosperity. It provides an opportunity to meet friends and relatives. It strengthens our social bonds and breaks the monotony of hectic and engrossed life.

35. Can you define festival, how is it celebrated and why is it celebrated?

Ans. Festivals act like vehicles that carry our culture, religion and history to a new generation. Well I must say, it is an occasion where everyone enjoy fun and fiesta. During festivals, we meet our friends, sit and share with them meals and laugh for long hours. It is celebrated as a symbol of our conventions and customs.

CULTURE

36. Do you think the culture of your country influences you?

Ans. Yes..I do… it reflects in your personality the way you eat, the way you dress, the way you adopt different lifestyles, its values and beliefs, etc. It is the widening of minds and spirits. It teaches you how unity can be maintained in the diversities of culture.

37. Which culture is the best, "Indian" or "Western"?

Ans. Well… culture never teaches you anything wrong. It is the thinking capacity of the person that allows you to think this is Indian or Western. The Indian culture is already enriched with values, and that's why it is incredible and the Western is completely based on Facts of those values, so I think no comparison exists between both of them. Both teaches the real virtues of life.

38. How has your countrys'culture changed in the last 50 years of time?

Ans. Change is the law of nature, but sometimes it's frightening to accept the change. Culture does not change because no doubt, it is accepted by the society in a different ways but its values and norms always remain the same. Earlier, it was limited to customs, now it is influencing our deportment, etiquettes, mannerisms, food habits. It would not be wrong to say it is our 'Signature's Style' these days.

LIFESTYLE, HEALTH, KEEPING FIT

39. Why do some people think that modern lifestyles are not healthy?

Ans. See, people have a valid reason for thinking so. People today love comfort and luxury and they want to satisfy their appetites at any cost. Rather than cooking at home, they love to eat out, at restaurants and fast food joints. Fast food may be tasty but contains a lot of fat that is not good for health. Previously, people used to walk or engage in some kind of manual work. That is not the case today. Personal vehicles and modern devices have made their life easy and people have great aversion towards sweating their bodies. This lifestyle naturally invites diseases.

40. Why do some people choose to lead unhealthy lives?

Ans. The simple answer is 'laziness'. Today many people do not have the discipline to lead a healthy life. They love comfort and convenience in everything that they do. In fact, they don't realise that their comfort and luxury are going to end soon. They need to face the reality sooner than later.

41. Should individuals or governments be responsible for making people lifestyles healthy?

Ans. It is the individuals themselves, who are responsible for making their lifestyles healthy. It is one's personal freedom to lead a healthy lifestyle. The government has nothing to do with it. No government can interfere into such personal affairs. Government can't ask people to eat this or that. The only thing that the government can do is to spread awareness about this issue. Nothing more than that.

42. What could be done to encourage people to live in a healthy way?

Ans. The best way to encourage people to live in a healthy way is to spread awareness about the consequences of an unhealthy lifestyle. This can be done through the media like television and newspapers. At an early age, children should be given education about the significance of a healthy lifestyle. It should also be included in the curriculum. Moreover, sports should be made compulsory in schools. Another effective way is to give gym and sports facilities in factories and offices.

MUSIC

43. Which instrument do you like to listen most? Why?

Ans. My favourite musical instrument is the *flute*. (I love listening to the flute, the most). I have always wondered why I like flute. Maybe, it is because of its simplicity or because of its sweet sound. Flute has a very soothing music and it goes directly into your heart. I think it is tough to learn flute, but I am not sure. Anyway, I like it.

44. Have you ever learnt to play a musical instrument?

Ans. Not really, I don't think I have the talent for it. So I have not seriously tried. When I was small, I just used to play with the harmonium, but actually, I could never play any proper notes. Even now, I love to press the keys of the electric keyboard and I like to hear the sound. But I have never learnt to play any musical instrument, though I love to listen to good and soft music.

CHILDREN'S GAMES

45. How have games changed from the time when you were a child?

Ans. Games have changed tremendously over the years. When we were children the standard of the game or the players was not as good as it is today. Moreover, newer rules have been introduced to make it more appealing to television audiences. I think the speed of the game has considerably increased. There is much more money in sports and games today, so more and more young people are interested in making it a full time career. That was not the case when I was a child.

46. Do you think this has been a positive change? Why?

Ans. Yes, it has definitely been a positive change in all ways. Games have become more popular and players get much better rewards. Televised games have made it possible for people to watch games in the comfort of their homes rather than going to a stadium. Watching games have become a very easy affair. Overall, the standard of the game has improved.

47. Why do you think children like playing games?

Ans. Children are physically very active and you can't keep them idle for a long time. They always like to be with their friends, playing some games. Psychologically, at their age, they can't think of engaging in a serious activity for a long time. Playing games would occupy them in a very effective way; otherwise, they are going to create some mischief at home.

BOOKS

48. What kind of books do you like to read?

Ans. I mostly like to read biographies. I'm not sure why, but it is interesting to read about people's real lives, especially when they have had interesting lives and have had to deal with many problems. I do read fictions as well, but I often find it difficult to get hold of a book that I really like. I also like reading about books on current affairs.

49. Do you read the same kind of books now that you read when you were a child?

Ans. Not really, no. Actually, I didn't read that much when I was a child, but if I did, it was mainly fiction books, such as fairy tales. Things like *The Lion, The Witch and the Wardrobe, Fantasy* things, etc.

50. When do you think is the best time to read?

Ans. I think any time is ok, but when I read, I like to concentrate, so I can't read for a short time like on a bus ride like some people do. I like to put time aside to enjoy it. So if I have some free time at the weekends, I might read for a few hours. And I nearly always read before I go to bed – this really helps me to get a sound sleep.

MOST POPULAR CUE-CARDS FOR IELTS TEST

CUE-CARD - 1 : LANGUAGE LEARNING

Let us talk about learning English

How long have you been learning English?

Where did you learn?

What is easy/difficult?

Is English important in your job?

I have been learning English ever since I was about 10 years old, when I was studying in my fifth grade. I learnt the alphabets and basic words at that time. I studied in a vernacular medium school, but English was a subject throughout my school years. I did not take English very seriously during my school days, and I scored comparatively poor marks for it. Well, English was the most difficult subject for me; and to be frank, I hated this subject at that time. One of the reasons that I did not like English was that we did not have any good teachers.

It was after I joined college, I began studying English seriously. I had a wonderful English teacher who laid a sound foundation in English Grammar. Since then, I started loving this subject and began reading books in English. Now I am in my forties and the more I study English the better I love it.

Since I am an English teacher, I need to improve my English all the time, learning new vocabulary and reading more and more books. I make sure that I update my knowledge of English all the time.

CUE-CARD - 2 : A GIFT THAT YOU PRESENTED

What was the gift?

What was the occasion?

Whom did you give it to?

Why was this gift very special?

My youngest brother was getting married and I wanted to give him a special gift. A couple of days before the marriage my wife and I went to the Shopping Mall for some shopping. As we were about to return, we just went to my favourite store, 'Wills Life Store'. In fact, this particular shop has the trendiest and the most fashionable clothes for both men and women. I had the gift in my mind when I went into the shop. After spending a few minutes in the store, I spotted an off-white linen casual shirt. It was a designer wear and I put it on to see how it looked. My wife said, 'It was the best shirt that had ever decorated my body. I was very happy. It was an expensive shirt, but it gave me a great sense of satisfaction'.

On the eve of the marriage, we had a party and my brother put this shirt on. Everybody was very appreciative of the shirt and my brother was very happy about it.

This gift was very special to me because I really liked the colour, material and the design of the shirt. Apart from that, it was first gift that I ever presented to my youngest brother. I was extremely happy that he really liked the shirt. It was the right occasion that I gave him this present.

CUE-CARD - 3 : A GIFT OR ARTICLE YOU TREASURE MOST

What was the article

Where did you get it?

How did you preserve it?

Why is it very precious to you?

Something that I treasure most is my IBM laptop, which was not actually a gift. Although it is quite old, it never had any serious technical problems, except a few software crashes, ever since I bought it about 8 years ago. Well, I bought it from a friend of mine who has a computer business. He suggested the brand and I think I made the right choice by buying an IBM laptop. Technically, the components of my computer are of very superior quality and therefore, in spite of my constant use, I have never changed any parts.

Although I have a leather laptop container, I rarely use it now. I used to put it in a leather bag initially, but later, due to my laziness, I just leave it on my study table. Sometimes, it gathers a lot of dust and occasionally, I wipe it with a towel. I would say my laptop is very untidily kept, but by God's grace it keeps working.

My laptop is very precious to me because I type my notes in it and use it for presentations in my class and meetings. Sometimes, I watch movies in it. I have also stored a lot of data and personal information in my computer. After my office hours, I spend a lot of time in front of my computer, either browsing the net or studying.

CUE-CARD - 4 : DESCRIBE A WEDDING YOU ATTENDED

You should say: when it was, who got married,
what happened at the wedding
And explain, whether it was a typical wedding ceremony

Happy and sad events are a part and parcel of our lives. The happy event I am going to talk about here is the wedding of my cousin. I attended this wedding on 15th January. My cousin name is Priya. She is my maternal aunt's daughter. All our friends and relatives were invited. Actually, the whole week before the 15th, I was busy in the pre-wedding celebrations like *Tilak, Sangeet, Mehandi, and Haldi*. On the day of the wedding, the marriage place was decorated like a bride. My cousin also looked beautiful in her sequin spangled *lehanga*. The *barrat* came at 5 p.m. High tea was served in which there were lots of cakes and snacks. Then there was the *Jai Mala*. The Bride and the Groom exchanged fresh flower garlands. Then we all danced and enjoyed to the beat of the music. After the sumptuous dinner, all the guests departed and only the close family member were left. Then the priest set a small fire and the remaining ceremony took place around the fire. The *Doli* was taken early in the morning. It was a very tearful moment for all of us but we were all happy from deep inside, as my cousin was beginning her new phase of life. Such celebrations are very common in my country.

CUE–CARD - 5 : DESCRIBE A GAME OR SPORT YOU ENJOY PLAYING

You should say:

- ★ What kind of sport is it?
- ★ With whom do you play?
- ★ Where do you play it and explain why you enjoy playing it

I enjoy playing various kinds of brain games online. There are a number of different websites I visit on a regular basis in order to play these games by myself. The objective of the games is to exercise different areas of your brain so that you preserve and enhance your memory and also expand and develop your brain capacity.

The games are of various kinds. Some enable you to practise your verbal skills. Others test your logical reasoning, spatial skills and visual memory. I can keep a track of my scores, so that each time I play, my goal is to do better than the past – to outdo myself, so to speak. In addition, if I want, I can compare my scores to others who play online. This aspect is intriguing, but frankly, it doesn't interest me much. I don't regard this as a competition with anyone else. It is something I do simply to sharpen my mental abilities and improve myself.

In fact, one of my favourite games is supposed to be the best for brain fitness. It involves solving a number of simple math problems using addition, subtraction, multiplication and division as quickly as possible. I really hope these games will enable me to preserve my intellect and my memory into old age.

CUE–CARD - 6 : DESCRIBE SOMEONE IN YOUR FAMILY WHOM YOU LIKE

You should say:

- ★ How is this person related to you?
- ★ How does this person look like?
- ★ What kind of person he/she is and explain why you like this person

The person in my family who I really like and also love is my mother. She is a very special person and I cannot imagine what I would be without her.

Physically, my mother is petite. She is only about 5 feet tall, and weighs about 110 pounds. She has fine, black hair and a fair complexion. One thing people often notice is that my mother always takes pride in her appearance. Even now, at the age of 80, my mother is a well dressed, well-groomed and an elegant woman, with her fine choice of clothes and matching accessories, jewellery and shoes.

Intellectually, my mother always loves learning. Even after her busy day, she won't go to bed without reading the newspaper. She was one of the few members of her family who completed the university education. She also has many creative and cultural interests such as literature, music and dance. Through her own enjoyment, she passed on this love of culture to all her children, including me.

Emotionally, my mother has a heart of gold. All her life, she has been ready, willing and able to help anyone who needs anything, with a smile on her face. She is of the old school – she remembers to wish friends and relatives on their birthdays and anniversaries, she attends their weddings, dinners and parties, and she visits them when they're hurt, unwell or in mourning. In fact, my mother has always been a kind soul and people of all ages love her as soon as they meet her. I think this is because she is good-hearted from her core, and her authenticity is what everyone relates to. She has taught me the meaning of being compassionate, loving, kind, helpful, supportive and so much more. In fact, thanks to the unconditional love of both my wonderful parents, I feel I've been truly blessed in this lifetime.

CUE-CARD - 7 : DESCRIBE YOUR FAVOURITE BOOK

You should say:

- ✯ Which book is it?
- ✯ Where did you read it?
- ✯ Why do you think it would be useful in future?

I have read many books in my life. In my view, books represent a way to get away from boredom of life and it helps me to be more creative by helping me exercise my own imaginations. Books also help me to increase my knowledge as well as vocabulary. It also enhances my reading skills.

The book, I would like to talk about here is 'THE SECRET'. It is written by Rhonda Byrne. She is a very famous writer. A movie has also been made after the success of this book. The secret contains wisdom of modern day teachers, men and women who have used it to achieve health, wealth and happiness. By applying the secret, they bring to light the compelling stories of eradicating diseases, acquiring massive wealth and overcoming obstacles.

They have achieved so many things which one would regard as impossible. In this book, you will learn how to use the secret in every aspect of life, i.e, money, health and relationships. You will begin to understand the hidden untapped power that's within you and this revelation can bring joy to every aspect of your life. There is also a very famous quote written in this book that if you really think of achieving something then the whole world conspires in your favour.

So I think I would definitely like to read this book again as it evokes positive feelings within me and every time, I feel motivated and revitalized whenever I go through this book. I would rather suggest my friends also to read this book.

CUE-CARD - 8 : TALK ABOUT A SITUATION WHEN YOU WERE ANGRY

- ✯ What was the situation?
- ✯ Where was it?
- ✯ Who was there?
- ✯ When was it?

Normally, I do not lose my temper easily. My friends say that I am as cool as a cucumber. However, there have been times when I was a little angry. I remember one such time when

I was angry with my friend.

I had to go for a job interview to Jalandhar, and I was very nervous. It was a walk-in-interview for a call centre job and I requested my friend, Roshni to accompany me. I somehow feel very confident when she is around.

She has a great sense of humour and never lets me feel sad or depressed. She also promised to accompany me but on the day of the interview, she did not turn up. Her phone was also switched off. I had to go alone.

I was very hurt and angry. I appeared for the interview and after coming back home, I went straight to her house. I wanted to shout at her and give her a piece of my mind. However, when I reached her home, I came to know that her father had taken ill suddenly and was admitted to the ICU. Her phone was also switched off because she was in the ICU attending her father. Everything had happened so suddenly that she did not get the time to call and inform me.

All my anger vanished and I felt ashamed of myself. I should have known that she would not ditch me for some trivial reason. I should have had more faith in her. This incident strengthened our ties of friendship even more.

CUE-CARD - 9 : TALK ABOUT YOUR FAVOURITE COLOUR

You may say:

- What colour is it?
- When this colour become important in your life
- Why does this colour matter to you?
- How does your choices get affected by this colour?

Colours are very important in everyone's life. It adds charm and spice to one's life. A world without colour would be dull and boring indeed! I like many colours such as red, blue, yellow, green and black. But my all time favourite is red. I don't exactly remember when this colour became important to me but once in school, I took part in a fancy dress competition and wore something in red.

Then I won the first prize. Since that day, I consider it my lucky colour. Even my school bag used to be red. Even today, my wardrobe is full of shades of red. This colour matters to me because I look good in red.

Whenever I wear red, I get many compliments. My choices are also affected by this colour. I buy accessories, such as bags, sandals and jewellery also in different shades of red. [For boys – My bike (car) is also of red colour] Red has a lot of importance in our culture. Hindu brides usually wear red. Red is also the symbol of love. It also symbolises danger. Red is also used as a vital traffic signal.

The colour of our blood is also red. Fire engines are red too! It is a primary colour. We can make many colours by mixing red – for example, we can make orange by mixing yellow with red. We can make pink by mixing white with red.Therefore, red is my favourite colour.

CUE-CARD - 10 : DESCRIBE AN OLD PERSON THAT YOU KNOW

You should say:

- ★ What is your relationship with this person?
- ★ How often do you see him?
- ★ What do people think about this person?
- ★ Explain why you like him.

Ok, I'd like to tell you about an old person that I know. His name is Harsh, and he is the owner of a small convenience store at the end of my street.

I would say that my relationship with him is as a friend. I know him because I regularly go to the shop in order to buy things when I don't have time to go to a supermarket. He's quite friendly and I always have a chat with him. Infact, I've known him now for about five years – since I've lived in this area. That's why, I'd now call him a friend.

I'd say that I see him fairly regularly. Like I said, I go to the big supermarket out of town sometimes to stock up, but you always need odd things during the week, such as milk, or some snack or other. So when this happens, I just have a walk down to his shop. Therefore, So I'd say I see him every day or every two days.

I think Harsh is pretty popular as he's been there for years as far as I'm aware, so most of the locals around the area know him. There will always be someone in the shop having a chat with him. They like him because he's not just the shopkeeper but he's also very involved in the local activities in the community. For example, I know he helps out at the old people's home some nights, and he runs the quizzes at the local pub. He also helps to organize the fair that is held each year in the town.

The reason that I like him is that he's great to have a chat with. For instance, a while back, I was having problems with my work, and I was really feeling stressed. I didn't really have anyone to talk to at the time as my family is abroad and a couple of my good friends were not around. I mentioned it to Harsh and he was great. He listened and also gave me some really good advice. Generally, he's really welcoming when you go to his shop. He always has a smile on his face.

CUE-CARD - 11 : Describe Your Favourite Dress

You should say:

★ What is it?

★ When did you buy it?

★ Why did you buy it and say why you like it so much?

There are various kinds of dresses which are available in the market that we can wear on different occasions but the dress which I think proved important for me was a party wear leather jacket with Italian designs on it. I got this jacket from Chandigarh when I went to my cousin's marriage function. That time I was taken for shopping in the famous market of Chandigarh where I could find the dresses of different brands with some warranty with them. So, I bought this jacket as I liked it most. This jacket was useful to me as I could use it to wear on my cousin's marriage and moreover, everybody praised it when I wore it on the marriage day. It had designing of some mirrors on it which fascinated everybody in the gathering and everybody praised my jacket and dressing sense.

Yes, of course, I can say this dress is very special for me now also as I sometimes wear it on some special occasions and also because it was helpful to me fetching some good words from the people present in my cousin's wedding about my dressing sense. So I like this dress very much.

CUE-CARD - 12 : DESCRIBE THE STAGE IN YOUR LIFE YOU HAVE ENJOYED MOST

You should say:

★ Which was stage it?

★ Why it was glorious?

★ How you enjoyed and say what lesson you learned.

Normally everybody passes through various types of situations comprising their weal or woe in life. I remember one stage of my life which was really enjoyable and full of fun for me which came in my childhood period and was my school days.

Yes definitely, these days were the enjoyable period of my life as I would get up in time and dress up and carry the bag already packed by my mother. Sometime my mother would help me in completing the work which I would get from my teacher in my school. So I can say I have no tension in those days and responsibilities were also not on my head. It was the gala time of my life in which I would meet my friends and enjoy their company when we would get together during the half time break in school and used to enjoy eating food together. This period was important for me as it taught me how we can work hard in the right direction to accomplish our goals or aims in life. Moreover this time gave me some lesson about friends that true friendship is based on loyalty and truth spoken by two friends to each other. So this was the most enjoyable time of my life.

CUE-CARD - 13 : DESCRIBE A PHOTOGRAPH THAT YOU REMEMBER

You should say:

- ✭ When was it taken?
- ✭ Who took it?
- ✭ What is in the photograph and explain why you remember this photograph?

I have a collection of many photographs in my album. Here I'm going to describe one such photograph in which I and my cousin are standing with our grandparents in our farmhouse. There is a small round table on which there is a cake. I remember vividly, it was the Golden Jubilee celebrations of my grandparents. My aunt baked and iced the cake at home. She's an expert cook. She only clicked the photo.

That's why she is not there in the picture. But her presence can be felt through the cake. Only the four of us were there in the picture. Last year, when I celebrated my parents Silver Jubilee, I wished in my heart that I celebrate their Golden Jubilee too. The table cloth which is spread on the table was embroidered by my grandma. She had a gifted hand in needle and thread work. Both my grandparents are no more in this world now. I really treasure this photograph as this brings nostalgic memories of my childhood. Now I have a digital camera in which I capture precious moments. Maybe, one day my children will value them.

CUE-CARD - 14 : DESCRIBE ANY HISTORICAL BUILDING YOU VISITED

You should say:

- ✭ What is it?
- ✭ Where is it located?
- ✭ What did you like in it and explain what is its significance in your country's history?

India is a diverse country. It has a rich historical background. The place I am going to talk about here is the Golden Temple or the Harmandir Sahib or the Temple of the God at Amritsar.

It is a place of stupendous beauty and sublime peace. It is situated at Amritsar in Punjab.The Sikhs all over the world daily wish to pay obeisance at Shri Harmandir Sahib. Although the 4th guru of Sikhs the Guru Ram Dal had the idea of this temple, but it was made by the 5th guru, Guru Arjan Dev ji. It took 16 years to complete this temple. The temple is surrounded with a large lake of water, known as *sarover* which consists of Amrit (holy water or immortal vector). There are four entrances which signifies openness and acceptance. People of all castes, creed, religion and sex are welcome here. However, everyone must cover his/her head as a mark of respect, remove their shoes and wash feet in the small pool of water. People from every nook and corner of the world flock to see the Golden Temple. I go there once a month to prostrate before the God. Whenever we have guests then a visit to the Golden Temple is surely on our agenda.

CUE-CARD - 15 TALK ABOUT ANY LAW OF YOUR COUNTRY

★ What is that law?

★ Why is it important?

★ When is it implemented and explain what steps have been taken to implement it?

There are various laws introduced or imposed by the government from time to time. All these laws are meant for the society. Otherwise, there will be the *Rule of Jungle* prevailing in the society where *Might is Right* is the slogan of every citizen and chaos and anarchy are the key words that represent its rule. The law I am going to talk about is PNDT, i.e, PRE NATAL DIAGNOSTIC TECHNIQUE ACT. This was first enforced in 1994 and then amended in 2002. In it, there is fine of Rs. 1 lakh, imprisonment and cancellation of licence and registration of the doctor who is caught doing the test.

It is a big disgrace to the Indian society which considers the birth of a girl child as a bad investment in the future. She is considered as a consumer than a producer that gives rise to the practice of female foeticide. The situation is quite worst in Punjab where sex ratio is 700 girls per 1000 boys. The decline in the sex ratio brings the degeneration of moral values resulting in red rafficking, polyandry, violence against women, etc. Undoubtedly, this law is implemented in a proper way, but is feared that these practices are going on the back street. Only this law is not sufficient, we should take some special measures to implement it, like providing old age pension to the old persons particularly, who don't have any son, free and compulsory education for the girls, job reservation for the girls, equal share of the girls in the property of parents. In the end, etc. I must say we all have to join hands to build a gender balanced society.

CUE-CARD - 16 : DESCRIBE A MAJOR DECISION YOU HAVE TAKEN IN YOUR LIFE

You should say:

- ✯ What was the decision?
- ✯ What other choices were available to you?
- ✯ Why did you take the decision and explain if you think that the decision was a good one.

A really important decision I've made recently is to study abroad. No one from my family has ever had the chance to do this before, and my parents were actually hoping I'd start working for the family textile business. I think it's too soon to join the business though. I really want to study marketing – especially *e-marketing* – so that I can contribute more to my parent's firm in the future. If I study e-marketing in the UK, I can learn how to use the internet to sell our clothes all over the world. As for whether it was the right decision, I'm pretty confident it was and I can't change my mind now anyway because my parents have borrowed money from my uncle to pay for my tuitions. I really can't wait to come back with new ideas that will help expand our business. All I need now is to get a good score in IELTS. So, anyway, that's an important decision in my life.

CUE-CARD - 17 : DESCRIBE AN ACTIVITY YOU LIKE DOING MOST

You should say:

- ✯ What is the activity?
- ✯ How often it you do?
- ✯ How does it help you forget your routine life?
- ✯ And say whether you would recommend other people try the same thing.

OK, I'd like to talk about horse-riding. I'm actually the joint owner of a horse with two of my friends and we take turns looking after it, cleaning out the stable and so on. I don't have a part-time job, so I spend most of my weekends at the stable. Taking care of a horse is quite a dirty business so it's obviously very different from studying at college. There's quite a large field next to the stable and I just get a wonderful sense of freedom when I'm riding around on my horse. The college seems a million miles away then! Do I think other people would enjoy horse-riding? Yes, absolutely. I think everyone should give it a try.

CUE-CARD – 18 : DESCRIBE A LANGUAGE YOU WOULD LIKE TO LEARN

You should say:

* What is the language?
* Where is it spoken?
* Why are you interested in this language?
* And say, if you think you will ever actually have the chance to learn it.

Let me tell you about a language I've always wanted to learn, which is Russian. It's spoken in Russia, obviously, but also in many other countries which have been influenced by Russia including places like Mongolia and Kazakhstan. The reason, I would like to learn Russian is that the energy industry is huge and there are lots of jobs in that industry. A lot of my country's oil and gas come from Russia; so it's really useful to be able to speak that language if you want to work in the energy field. And I know that a lot of Russians can't speak English very well, so there's another reason to learn their language. The problem is I'm already in my thirties and I've spent more than ten years learning English. I don't know if I would ever be able to study Russian because it uses a completely different alphabet and sounds really difficult. But it would be really nice to have the chance to learn it.

CUE-CARD – 19 : TALK ABOUT A JOB THAT HELPS TO MAKE THE WORLD A BETTER PLACE

You should say:

* What job is it?
* Where did you learn about it?
* Why do you think it helps so much?

There are many jobs in the world which help to make the world a better place, such as the job of a teacher, a doctor, a nurse, a scientist, a politician and so many more. In fact, the world can be made better by the cumulative effort of all these jobs. Here I would like to talk about a job which helps to make the world a better place. This is the job of a teacher.

Everyone passes through the hands of teachers in school and college years. *Teachers* are known as *nation builders*. All other professions, also pass through the hands of a teacher. *That is why I believe that teachers can make the world a better place.* A teacher is like a candle that burns itself and shows light to others. Since age-old times, *teaching has been considered a noble profession*. In ancient India, there was the *Gurukul system*. Even the king's children stayed in the homes of the gurus or the teachers. They used to do the household chores of the guru and in return the guru imparted knowledge.

Teachers improve the literacy rate of a country. When literacy rate is high, crime and violence go down. A teacher requires good communication skills and depth of knowledge of his subject.

A good teacher should treat all students equally. Nowadays, teachers are being paid handsomely by the government. This is to lure bright students to join this profession.

CUE-CARD – 20 : DESCRIBE A PIECE OF FURNITURE IN YOUR HOUSE

(The wording might include "that you often use")

You should say:

★ What is it?

★ Where is it?

★ What it looks like (or, what it is made of) and explain how or why you use it.

Furniture is a part and parcel of every home. There is a lot of furniture in my home too. There are beds and sofa sets, chairs and tables, cupboards and dressing tables. But here I would like to talk about a piece of furniture that I use very often. This is a study table.

I have this table in my room. This is a special table which my father got made for me by a carpenter in my hometown. The body of the table is made of pure teak wood. The top is of board which has a grey mica topping. This is bigger than a conventional study table.

It is L – shaped. On one side, I have set my desktop PC.There are shelves on the top on which I have set my books. There are drawers on one side in which I keep my stationery materials CDs and DVDs. A chair can be slid inside the table when not in use.

I find this table very convenient when I have to study or work on my computer. I have a beautiful table lamp on one side. The light falls on my books from the left side. I just love this table. So, this is one important item of furniture in my house.

CUE-CARD – 21 : TALK ABOUT A PLACE YOU HAVE VISITED AT OPEN AIR

You should say:

★ Where did you go?

★ Why did you go there?

★ What did you do there?

I have visited many places in the open air, such as parks and stadiums. But here I would like to talk about the rock garden in Chandigarh. I went there with my college/school trip last year. Our school/college organised an educational tour to Chandigarh. We were 30 students and two teachers.We saw many places, such as the *Rose Garden, Sukhna Lake, Mini Zoo* and the Rock Garden. The Rock Garden by Nek Chand fascinated me the most. We spent two hours there and clicked a lot of photographs. About 5000 people(tourists) visit the Rock Garden daily.

It has around 5000 sculptures. It is a unique garden that consists of various art objects.

But the best part about the Rock Garden is that each of its artwork has been made by using waste materials. The Rock Garden has become immensely popular. It has been established in the form of an open-air exhibition hall.

The garden has sculptures made by using a variety of different discarded waste materials like frames, mudguards, forks, handle bars, metal wires, play marbles, porcelain, auto parts, broken bangles, etc.

The garden highlights the value of materials many people consider trash. People come from different parts of the world to see this amazing garden. It is located in Sector 1 near the Sukhna Lake. Nek Chand received the Padam Shri in 1983 for his efforts. A sculpture of this garden also appeared on an Indian postage stamp.

The Chandigarh Rock Garden is now acknowledged as one of the Modern Wonders of the World.

CUE-CARD – 22 : TALK ABOUT A SITUATION IN YOUR LIFE THAT MADE YOU LAUGH FROM YOUR HEART.

You should say:

- ★ What was the occasion?
- ★ When was it held?
- ★ Who witnessed it with you and why did it make you laugh?

It has been rightly said that laughter is the best medicine. Unfortunately, in the fast paced hectic lifestyle of today we are forgetting to realise the importance of this free medicine. Even doctors are recommending this therapy for many depressive disorders.

Nowadays, people have again begun to realise its importance. No wonder, we can see many sitcoms on TV nowadays, such as *Comedy Circus* and *Chhote Miyan. Laughter Clubs, etc.,* which have also opened in many cities where people come to laugh out their worries and stress. I have also faced many situations when I burst into peals of laughter.

Here I would like to talk about one such situation when I really laughed from my heart.

It was my cousin's wedding two months ago and we were all dancing on the beats of DJ. The groom's father, that is my uncle had taken a few pegs of whiskey. He was dancing the maximum. His odd and weird dancing steps were very hilarious and everyone was laughing at him. But he was not at all perturbed. He was thoroughly enjoying himself.

My aunt tried to stop him many times but he wouldn't listen. He was wearing a silken *dhoti kurta*. Suddenly, he tripped and his *dhoti* came off. That was the most hilarious moment of all. The bride and the groom also had a hearty laugh. The photographer captured it all very nicely in his video camera.

Even today, when we see that video we all have a hearty laugh.

CUE-CARD - 23: AN ADVERTISEMENT THAT CAUGHT YOUR ATTRACTION

You should say:

- ✯ Which advertisement is it?
- ✯ Why do you like it?
- ✯ What is this advertisement all about and explain what message it wants to convey.

You know, now some commercials are better than the TV programmes. In the past, we did not have so many TV commercials. Now, we have a plethora of them – before, in the middle and after each program. I think TV commercials add variety to the program because sometimes the program becomes very monotonous.

Some TV commercials also give you a chance of refreshment. The TV advertisement I am going to talk about here is of *Vodaphone Telecom*. It is a very humorous commercial. A 6-7 years old girl is shown to be getting ready for school. She can't find her socks. Her very cute puppy obliges by finding her socks. Then she is shown sitting in her school bus. She has forgotten her school tie. Then they show the cute puppy running after the bus with the tie around its neck.

What the vodaphone people want to convey is that their network follows wherever they go. They also want to show that they are always willing to help. I changed my phone connection from cell-one to vodaphone after seeing this advertisement. Cell-one was giving me a lot of problems with network, but now I have no such problems.

CUE-CARD - 24 : YOUR FAVOURITE CUISINE

You should say:

- ✯ Which dish is it?
- ✯ How is it made?
- ✯ Who made it and explain where it is available.

I like all cuisines, such as Chinese, Indian and Mexican, but my all time favourite is the Indian cuisine. The Indian cuisine has a lot of diversity. The North Indian and the South Indian cuisines are poles apart. Although I like both, but I really relish North Indian cuisine. Green vegetables, pulses, lentils and a variety of desserts are part of the North Indian cuisine.

My favourite dish is *Makki di Roti* and *sarson da saag*. Actually, *makki di roti* is a loaf made of maize flour and *sarson da saag* is a dish made of mustard leaves to which spinach leaves can be added. My mother cooks very delicious *saag*. It is a winter dish but now you can eat the tinned *saag* at any time of the year. Good marked companies market the tinned variety.

CUE-CARD 25 : MY FAVOURITE SHOPPING MALL

You should say:

- ✯ Which mall is it?
- ✯ How does it looks like?
- ✯ What type of stores and explain who maintain it

Many new shopping malls have come to view recently in my hometown. The Arjun Mall and Ansal Plaza are the two major ones. Here I am going to talk about the Ansal Plaza.

It is in the suburbs of Phagwara. It is a modern shopping mall built with the state-of-the-art technology.

Ansal Plaza has four storeys. It has a huge parking in the basement that can hold more than a 100 cars. Ansal Plaza has escalators and 4 lifts. The Plaza has 3-4 food courts including McDonalds which is my favourite place to eat out.

The Ansal Plaza is a joint venture of some businessmen of Delhi and has many branches in India.

It is on the highway and is always flocked by countless hordes of people. It also has many branded stores like Reebok and Nike.

CUE-CARD - 26 : YOUR FAVOURITE PLACE OF EATING OUT

Describe a restaurant you know.

You should say:

- ✯ Where is this restaurant?
- ✯ What type of food does the restaurant serves?
- ✯ How often do you visit this restaurant and explain why you would recommend this restaurant.

There are many restaurants which I visit frequently but here I am going to describe the *Haveli*.

It is on the National Highway between Jalandhar and Phagwara. Basically, it falls in the suburbs of Phagwara.

I like it because of the delicious and quality food, quick and prompt service and a friendly atmosphere. It is always swarming with people and brimming with activity.

The food is priced at very normal rates. It is a huge place with a seating capacity of about 200 people. The interior is decorated to simulate a traditional Punjabi village scene. Handicrafts adorn the walls which give the place a very ethnic look. The food served is mouth watering and delicious. The restaurant is very clean and hygienic.The waiters are amicable and friendly.

In the evenings Punjabi cultural songs & dances are performed by various artists.

It is a must-visit place for one and all. It is so interesting that one can never feel bored there.

CUE-CARD - 27: YOUR FAVOURITE MAGAZINE/PERIODICAL/ JOURNAL

DESCRIBE A MAGAZINE YOU THINK IS INTERESTING

You should say:

- ✯ Why do you like this magazine?
- ✯ What are its salient features?
- ✯ What does it contain and explain why you think this magazine is interesting.

My favourite magazine is ‘The Reader’s Digest’. It is a monthly international magazine. The editor of the magazine is Mohan Sivanand. I like this magazine because it is not a magazine to be read and thrown away. It is informative and thought-provoking.

I have collected many past issues of the magazine in my personal library. There are many regular features of the magazine. The feature I like the most is ‘word power’.

It gives me 20 new words of English every month with their meanings and antonyms.

It helps me to improve my vocabulary tremendously.

The other regular features are – ‘laughter is the best medicine’, ‘life is like that’ and ‘humour in uniform’. All these articles contain jokes and humours which are always fresh. There are also many quotable quotes in this magazine.

Another article I like is ‘The reader’s choice’. It runs for 15-20 pages. It contains a true story or an abridged form of a novel. All these articles are very inspiring.

Reading this magazine relaxes me. This magazine is entertaining and educative. Everybody in my house reads it. This magazine has something for everybody.

CUE-CARD - 28 : YOUR FAVOURITE NEWSPAPER

You should say:

- ✭ Why do you like this newspaper?
- ✭ What are its salient features?
- ✭ What it contains and explain why you think this newpaper is interesting.

There are many newspapers published in my city in different languages. My parents have subscribed to one Punjabi newspaper *Ajeet* and one English newspaper, i.e., *The Tribune* I like to read The Tribune. It is a complete newspaper according to me.

It has many pages that cover important topics, national and international news and also local news from my state and city. The editor's page is called the 'Opinion'. I read the editorial daily.

It touches topics of daily interest. Different social, political and international topics are discussed in this section.

Only the other day, I read about *global warming*. There is a supplement every alternate day.

On Wednesday, it is *Jalandhar Plus*. In this supplement, local news of my hometown *Phagwara* is also there. I have been reading this newspaper for quite some time now. I don't think there is any room for improvement, but then *a technology section* would add a feather in the cap of this paper.

CUE-CARD - 29 : YOUR FAVOURITE CHANNEL

You should say:

- ✭ Which channel do you like?
- ✭ What are its features?
- ✭ Why do you like it and explain what you learn from this channel?

Nowadays there is a multitude of channels and a plethora of programmes on TV.

As I am an animal lover, my favourite channel is *Animal Planet*. Animal Planet is a very informative channel.

I like this channel because I have learnt a lot from this channel. It provides me with a new word of English every 20 minutes.So it has improved my vocabulary a lot. It is an offshoot of the *Discovery Channel*. My favourite programme is *Animal Safari*. You can learn about animals, birds and reptiles from it. This channel can never be boring. Some programmes are real eye-openers.

I learnt many facts about the animal world from this channel.

CUE-CARD - 30 : YOUR FAVOURITE ANIMAL

You should say:

- ★ Which animal do you like?
- ★ Why do you like?
- ★ Where does it reside and explain its lifestyle.

The animal I like the most is the *elephant*. The elephants are the biggest land animals. They are *herbivorous* and can be identified because of their trunks. The trunk is the projection of their noses and the upper lips. There are two types of elephants – the *Indian* and the *African*. African elephants are bigger than their Indian counterparts.

They have comparatively larger ears. Among the African elephants, both the males and females have tusks, whereas, only the males among the Indian elephants have tusks and so they are called *tuskers*.

The back of the Indian elephants are *convex,* whereas that of the African elephants are *concave*. The Indian elephants can be tamed and they are more beautiful. Elephants are gregarious animals and live in herds headed by the tuskers. They have a well-structured family life. The young ones, called the calf, are looked after by the cow elephants. Their cry is called the *trumpet*.

In India, elephants are captured, tamed and used for various purposes.

Elephants are among the few animals whose existence are not endangered till now.

CUE-CARD - 31 : YOUR FAVOURITE POET

You should say:

- ★ Which poet he/she is?
- ★ What do you like in his/her personality?
- ★ His/her talent features and explain his/her works

My favourite poetess is *Amrita Pritam*. She's no more now. She died at the age of 86 on 31st October, 2005. She was a charismatic personality. She was very beautiful with almond-shaped eyes, fine features and a fair complexion.

She began composing poetry in her teens. Amrita's father was a man of letters and encouraged Amrita to read and write. She published her first book of poems when she was just fourteen.

After the Partition in 1947, Delhi became her home. Her talent blossomed in the capital of independent India, and writing in Punjabi, her mother tongue, she was to take the language places. Her poem *Aaj Aakhaan Waris Shah Noo* made her reach the pinnacles of fame. She often wrote on the condition of Indian women and her writings reflected their neglect and suppression in Indian society.

She has to her credit 15 novels, numerous short stories and poems. She witnessed the Partition of India and portrayed it in her works. Her works have been widely translated. She has received many awards, including India's highest literary award, Jnanpith, in 1981. Films have been made on two of her novels – Daaku and Pinjar (skeleton). Her other famous novels are: Kachchi Sarak (HINDI), Lal Dhagee ka Rishta HINDI)Raseedi Ticket (HINDI), The Revenue Stamp – An Autobiography. Her other famous poems are Khamoshi Se Pahle (HINDI) Aawazen (HINDI).

CUE-CARD - 32 : YOUR FAVOURITE FILM STAR

You should say:

- ✯ Which Filmstar he/she is
- ✯ What you like in his personality
- ✯ His/her talent features and explain his/her works

I like many film stars like Shah Rukh Khan, Aamir Khan, Salman Khan but here I am going to talk about Amitabh Bachhan. He is my all-time favourite.

He is a versatile actor and really lives the role he is given. He is the Shehanshah of Bollywood and the superstar of the millennium. He is an apple of the eye of millions of Indians. He has appeared in more than 180 films. His debut film 'Saat Hindustani' did not succeed in the box office but his 1970s films Zanjeer, Deewar and Sholay took him to the pinnacle of his career.

He met with a near-fatal accident while shooting for Coolie in 1983.

He has a strong will power. He took ill once again in 2005 and underwent a major surgery of intestine but again recovered because of his will power. He has won many awards. He has even hosted a TV show, KBC (Kaun Banega Crorepati)

He is a legend.There is no one else who can replace this legend. I like his movie Baghban the most.

CUE-CARD - 33 : A STORY YOU HAVE HEARD AS A CHILD

You should say:

- ★ Which story it is
- ★ What is the story all about?
- ★ Why do you like it and explain what moral lesson you have learnt from it.

The story I've heard as a child is of a thirsty crow. Once upon a time, there was a crow. The crow was very intelligent. One day, it felt very thirsty. It wanted to quench its thirst. It looked for water everywhere. But nowhere could it find the water. Then it found a pitcher with a little water at the bottom.

The crow could not reach the water. It pondered and immediately hit upon an idea. It gathered pebbles and dropped them into the pitcher. The water level rose. It drank the water and quenched its thirst. It's very easy to learn and one of the most popular stories during childhood days. The moral of the story is that at the time of adversity, you've to use your wits.

CUE-CARD - 34 : YOUR LAST DAY AT SCHOOL

You should include:

- ★ Which day was it
- ★ How did you celebrate?
- ★ What did you do and explain how it became memorable for the whole of your life.

An unforgettable incident in your school days and in your life. My last day at school was a very memorable one. I remember vividly the date also. It was the 6th of February. Our juniors had organised a farewell party for us. We all were very excited about that day. In fact, most of us had bought new clothes for that day. Our principal and all the teachers were also invited.

Our juniors had many surprises for us up their sleeves. They also had many awards for us. We all were asked to perform on the stage. It could be a *mono-acting* or a *joke* or a *song or dance*. Everyone was doing rather well. When my turn came, I became very nervous. It was stage fright. I had never performed on the stage before. My legs were shaking. As I went up the stage, I tripped and fell face down on the stage.

Everyone burst into pearls of laughter. It was the most embarrassing moment for me.

I too started laughing. I realised that if you have the courage to laugh at yourself others don't laugh at you anymore and that's the best way to overcome embarrassment. I told them all a joke. As I started speaking, I realised that all my nervousness flew away and everyone enjoyed my performance.

Guess what? I won the best boy/girl award too! It was the happiest moment of my life and the most unforgettable one too! We had a lot of refreshments too and danced a lot on that day.It was very painful.

CUE-CARD - 35 : YOUR FAVOURITE FESTIVAL

You should say:

- ✯ Which festival it is
- ✯ Why do you like this festival?
- ✯ How is it celebrated and explain what activities are prominent during this festival

Diwali or Deepawali is a Hindu festival of lights.The word, Deepawali literally means rows of *diyas* (clay lamps). It is a family festival. It is celebrated 20 days after Dussehra. It is celebrated to commemorate the return of Lord Rama to his kingdom after 14 years of exile. It is also meant to celebrate the destruction of the arrogant tyrant Bali at the hands of Vishnu.

Another reason for the celebration of Diwali is that the 6th guru of the Sikhs, Guru Hargobind Ji, was set free from Gwalior jail along with 52 kings on this day.

During Diwali twinkling oil lamps or *diyas* light up every home and there are numerous firework displays. Lord Ganesha, the elephant-headed God, the symbol of auspiciousness and wisdom, is worshipped in most of the Hindu homes.

Goddess Lakshmi, who is the symbol of wealth and prosperity, is also worshipped. Spring cleaning and whitewashing of houses are done. *Rangolis* (decorative designs) are painted on the walls and the floors. New clothes are bought and family members and relatives gather together to offer prayers, distribute sweets and to light up their houses.

There are some bad practices also followed on this day. Some people resort to drinking and gambling which is not good.

CUE-CARD - 36 : A VISIT TO A MUSEUM

- ✯ When did you visit it?
- ✯ Describe the museum.
- ✯ How did you feel after going there?

Last month, my cousins came over to my house and they were insisting on going to a museum. I was not interested in going to the museum because I do not like museums at all. They finally persuaded me to go there and when I entered the museum, I was mesmerized by its beauty!

The museum was divided into sections. The first section was related to the great inventions, whereas the other section was mainly concerned with the paintings and all other stuff. I was more inclined towards the inventions, so I went to the first section. As I entered the area, I could see a huge computer. The computer was made in 1960s and it was of the size of a room. I was amazed to see its size and I realized that the computer engineers of today would have made a lot of effort to reduce the size of the computer. I also saw the first bulb and other stuff.

My cousin came to me and told that there was some interesting stuff down there on the other section, so I decided to give it a look. The other section consisted of paintings of the Mughal era. The paintings were very beautiful and they were depicting the beauty of that period. There was also a huge food court in the museum, so we went to eat something.

The overall experience of the museum was simply fantastic. I saw a lot of things and I came to know about my country's culture. I think that if I had not visited the museum, I would have regretted this decision for the rest of my life. I feel that everyone should pay a visit to a museum because it keeps him or her well informed about the culture and we should all applaud the efforts of our ancestors as they made many sacrifices to make our life easier.

CUE-CARD - 37 : THE SADDEST MOMENT IN MY LIFE

- What had happened?
- How did it change your life?
- How did you cope with it?

I have had a lot of sad moments in my life but the saddest moment in my life is when I failed in my Math exam. It was in grade 9. I was struggling a lot with my Math, so my father came to my rescue and he taught me. He used to teach me well but I never revised the concepts. I got 39% in the math exam and I came back home. My father asked me about the result as he had great expectations from me, but I told him that I had failed the exam.

At that moment, I saw his face, almost blacken suddenly showing as if he was blaming himself for my failure. He did not even scold me and went straight in to his room. That moment I realized that not taking my studies seriously was not only hurting me, but also my parents. I did not make any fake promises this time and I made a true promise to myself that no matter what happens I will work very hard for my exams and will try my best to achieve good grades in the exams.

I stopped watching movies and began concentrating on my studies. I don't know what was happening. I was getting a kind of strength to work harder and I was fully determined to show to the world that I was capable of something good and ultimately, I passed the next math exam with an A grade.

CUE-CARD - 38 : YOUR FAVOURITE MUSIC

- ★ What kind of music do you like?
- ★ When do you listen to it?
- ★ How does it change your mood?

Music is a very important part of every human being's life. Some people like hip hop, some people like rap and others like jazz. Different people have different tastes for music but there is one thing common amongst all these people, which is that almost everyone in this world is madly in love with music.

I am very fond of music. I like all types of music, but my favourite type of music is Indian music. I like to listen to sad Indian songs because I feel that I can relate to them. My life has not worked according to the plan and I have been sad for most part of my life. So I think that these songs are made for me.

I really like the songs in which the piano is played. I also know how to play the piano so I also play the same tunes on my own piano.

As I told you earlier that if I am sad I listen to sad songs so that I could become more sadder, but when I am happy I do not listen to sad song, on the contrary I listen to happy songs which make me more happy. So I would say that sad songs make me sadder whereas happy songs make me happier. Once recalled a day when I was sad and my cousin turned on a rap song and it actually infuriated me and I went out of the room, banging the door.

CUE-CARD - 39 : MEANS OF COMMUNICATION

- ★ Different means of communication
- ★ What is your favourite means of communication?
- ★ What are the advantages and disadvantages of using it?

Communication is very important to impart information from one person to another. In the medieval times people used to communicate via birds, signs and fire. Now the means of communication have changed, but the purpose of communication is the same. Languages were made to facilitate communication and people learnt languages to make communication better.

There are many means of communication in this world. I would like to tell you about the means of communication which I use. I use phone, laptop, e-mails and letter. I personally feel that mobile phone is the best means of communication. I remember that once I met with an accident and I was travelling alone in a rainy night. I did not know what to do, but I had my phone and I straight away called for help and I was able to get the help because of the phone.

There are many advantages of using a mobile phone as I mentioned earlier that it can help a person in emergencies other than that the phones are operating as mini-computers as they have all the features which are available in a computer. We can catch up with a friend without actually meeting the friend personally. Mobile phones tend to save time if they are used properly, for instance if I have to cancel a class I simply sends a message to the students and they come to know that I won't attend class today. This would apply if you are a teacher.

There are also some disadvantages of using mobile phone. The most obvious ones are that people waste a lot of time and money by talking on the phone for hours. I also hate the ring tones of mobiles, so I mostly keep my mobile silent.

CUE-CARD - 40 : MEANS OF TRANSPORTATION

- ★ Means of transportation in urban and rural areas your country?
- ★ Which means of transportation do you generally use?
- ★ What are the advantages and disadvantages of using it?

There are many means of transportation in my country. People in the urban areas usually have their own cars or they use the public transports, whereas people in the rural areas tend to travel on bicycles and tractors. People in this world use those means of transportation which are suitable for them. The previous mentioned means of transportation are used to travel within the country whereas the airplanes are used to travel from one county to another.

My favourite means of transportation is a car. I got this car when I was 19 years old. First I used to travel by a bus, but after getting the car my life got a lot of easier and felt that car was a necessity rather than a luxury. First I used to travel by bus and never reached my destination on time. There was a day when I missed a bus and due to that I also missed my exam so I got a zero in my exam. I think that the use of a car enables a person to reach on time and it also protects a person from bad weather. There are also some disadvantages attached to the use of car as it is very expensive to keep a car and a person also has to pay for the maintenance charges. Cars also create a lot of pollution and traffic congestion.

I still feel that the benefits of using a car outweigh the drawbacks, and more and more people in this world are trying to get their own cars.

CUE-CARD - 41 : UNIFORM

- ★ Why do people wear uniform?
- ★ Have you ever worn a uniform?
- ★ What role does uniform play in a person's life?

We all have seen people wearing uniform. People of different professions wear uniforms in order to distinguish them from other people and to show unity. You can easily observe that different organizations have different uniforms. I personally like the uniform of lawyers. Lawyers wear a black coat in my country which is looking quite good. Apart from lawyers there are also other people who wear uniforms. The most obvious ones are army men, doctors, students, police men and people of other law enforcement agencies.

I used to wear a uniform when I was in my school. I used to wear a white shirt and black pant. I was totally not cool with it. I always thought that my school should have allowed all the students in my school to wear of their chain clothes. I never felt good after wearing the uniform and I wanted to just take it off. But now that I am an adult I realize how wise it was of the school to make us wear these clothes. Wearing a uniform just saves us from the effort to try so hard to choose the clothes. Now I contemplate the idea behind making the students wear uniform. There are some rich and poor people in a school, so the schools introduce a uniform to promote equality and brotherhood amongst them. Uniform plays a vital role in the life of a person. It promotes unity, discipline and integrity. I can easily say that uniform has played a very imperative role in my life.

CUE-CARD - 42 : TYPES OF MOVIES YOU LIKE

You should say:

- ★ What type of movies do you like?
- ★ Compare different types of movies.
- ★ How do you feel after watching them?

I like to watch sad movies. I know that people would consider me as sadist, but I feel good after watching them. I am mostly interested in watching sad Indian movies. I feel that no one does sad movies better than the Indians and the songs make the entire thing a very unique experience. Two days ago, I watched two sad Indian movies and both of them were of Shah Rukh Khan. The actor acted well in both the films.

I go for movies every week with my friends and all of them are interested in action movies. So, after repeated requests, I decided to watch the movie and in the end, I was bored to death. The action was so childish and all people were jumping over buildings as if they were spiderman. It was pathetic and I think that I would never been able to adopt a liking for action movies as I am so much into sad movies.

I also watch action movies, but I an unable to connect my feelings with those movies. I got bored after 30 minutes, but there was a whole different story with sad movies. My life has been sad lately. I feel that I am able to relate myself to those movies and I endeavour to find a pattern which matches my lifestyle. I know this might be sounding crazy but it is how I feel about the thing.

CUE-CARD - 43 : MY FAVOURITE MOVIE

- ★ Name of your favourite movie.
- ★ Why do you like it so much.
- ★ What message does the movie convey?

I watch a lot of movies and this is the thing which I do in my leisure time. I love to watch movies and there are some movies which I watch again and again. My favourite movie is *The Terminal*. I have watched this movie many times, and I am not exaggerating it. I loved the way Tom Hanks acted in the movie and it was a very well executed movie. The movie is about a person who gets stuck in an airport and he has to live over there for months because the authorities do not let him go outside of the airport. Tom Hanks plays a character of a person who comes to America to fulfil his father's last wish and due to some reason he is unable to do what he has to do.

In the movie, Tom hanks lands at the airport and at the same time, there is a mutiny in his country and America stops recognizing his country. The movie shows how a person survives all these months and fulfils the wish of his dead father. There is a scene in the movie when the authorities ask him to say that he is afraid of his country, but he says no.

You would not believe what I am going to tell you now. Once I was travelling and I was stuck in Schipol Airport for 2 days. I had to face a similar kind of situation because my ticket had expired. I just felt as if the whole movie was going to be played again and I was to play the main character this time.

The movie shows that no matter what happens, a person should never compromise on his or her love for his country. The movie also gives a message that no matter how long the wait is, people with strong determination always achieve their goals.

CUE-CARD - 44 : AN INCIDENT THAT CHANGED MY LIFE

★ What happened?

★ Who was involved in it?

★ How did it change your life?

It was about 3 years ago when I was going to my friend's house. I was driving the car really fast. Speed always thrilled me and I always felt good by driving the car very fast, so I was driving the car fast when a car passed by me. It was faster than me and I reckon it would be travelling at a speed of 200km/hr. First I thought, I was going at the same speed but then I stopped. After about 30 seconds, I saw that the car had hit a truck and the driver of that car was lying dead.

I was not directly involved in the accident, but it had an overwhelming effect on my life. It changed everything. I never took life seriously and I never considered driving to be a hazardous activity, but the killing of the person had a devastating effect on my life. I realized that the thing which I considered to be fun could even take my life away and could destroy others too!

I made a strong resolution that day that I would end this kind of behaviour and try to avoid these things. I thought that doing this stuff could also take another person's life for which I would have never been able to forgive myself.

Now when ever I drive, my car, it is at a slow speed, and even if I have to reach a place urgently, I decide to drive slow because it is better to reach late than never.

CUE-CARD - 45 : THE HAPPIEST MOMENT IN MY LIFE

★ Describe it.

★ Why do you regard it as the happiest moment?

★ How did it affect your life?

The happiest moment in my life was when I passed my Grade 12. It was a crazy day. I was behaving like a maniac as I was so stressed out. I had to go to my school to get my results and I was panicking. My admission in the college was solely dependent on whether I pass or fail the exam, so it was very important for me to pass the exam.

I reached my school and I was trembling with fear because I thought that I would fail in one of the subjects. After a long wait, I was asked to pick my result and with trembling hands, I opened the envelope.

I had passed the exam. It was the happiest moment of my life. The main reason for the happiness was that I had not worked hard for the exam, but still I passed it. Somewhere in my heart I thought, that I did not deserve the passing marks, as getting it had almost no effort.

If I compare this situation to other events in my life, I can say that I have had better marks in other exams, but this was the most important one. After getting the HSD, I got admission in the college and I began my higher studies. I remember that most of the students in my class had not gotten it and they had to sit for the make-up exam; however, I was damn lucky and it also helped me realize that luck was not always going to work and in the future, I will have to put up some real efforts to achieve success in life.

CUE-CARD - 46 : THE MOST EMBARRASSING MOMENT IN MY LIFE

- ★ Describe the event.
- ★ Why did you feel so much embarrassed?
- ★ Can we avoid these kinds of incidents?

The most embarrassing moment in my life was when I went to school without my book. I was studying really hard all night. Actually, I was pulling an all-nighter, and I forgot to bring my books to school. As I was sitting in the class, my Math teacher asked all the students to take their books out, and as the students were taking their book out, the principal entered the class.

I put my hand in the bag and I realized that I had forgotten the book at home. Everyone in the class had brought the books and I was the only one who had not brought the book. The principal approached and asked me that why had I not brought the books? I told him that I was studying late, so I forgot the books in the house. He said to me that the only reason you have to study at home is that you do not bring your books to school and you do not study over here. It was such an embarrassing moment for me that I felt like crying. The entire class started laughing at me and I was the new dumbo of the class.

I do not think that we can avoid these embarrassing moments in our life. They are beyond our control as in my situation, my hard work for the night was not acclaimed and a slightest mistake just turned out to be a blunder and I had to face embarrassment in front of the whole class. Some people say that we can avoid certain things to avoid these incidents, but I do not think in a similar way.

CUE-CARD - 47 : MY FAVOURITE ELECTRONIC DEVICE

★ Name of the device

★ When do you use it?

★ How do other people regard this device?

My favourite electronic device is a laptop. I am not exaggerating by saying that I cannot live without it. When I did not have it I never thought it would become such an important thing in my life, but when I started using it, I realized that I could not live without it. I use a *Dell laptop* and it is very beautiful. Apart from being beautiful, it has a lot of functions and features which have made my life easier.

I carry my laptop all the time. The main reason, I use the *laptop* is that I am running my own website and for that reason, I have to look at the website statistics at all times. If I do not use my laptop, I would not be able to operate my website. I also use the laptop when I have to talk to my friends or when I have to check the e-mails. I have some friends who live in other cities so when I feel that I am missing them, or I feel that I should keep in touch with them then I talk to them on skype.

A laptop is an electronic device which has not only made my life better, but also the lives of many people better. People have been able to communicate in a much better and faster way and the communication done via the laptop or internet is almost free. At first, it was considered to be a luxury, but thanks to the modern technology, it has now become affordable for everyone.

CUE-CARD - 48 : YOUR FAVOURITE SPORTS EVENT

★ When and Why did you attend it?

★ Describe the sports event you attended.

★ What was the best part about the sports event?

It was about 9 years ago when I went to the Annual Sports Day of a school. It was a very grand event; more than 600 students were participating in different games. I had to attend it because my cousin was playing in the hockey team. I had come to watch the hockey match because I wanted to support my cousin.

It was a magnificent event. Things were organized incredibly well and the head boy of the school was organizing everything by himself. I was really impressed by the look of the event and it would not be wrong to compare the event to Olympics. There was a massive display of fireworks at the beginning of the hockey match and then the teams came for the match. I must say that it was a very interesting encounter.

The best of the sports event was when my cousin scored the goal. He had been working really hard to get a place in the team, and when he used this opportunity in the best way by scoring the only goal of the match. The entire crowd was cheering for my cousin, and it was a moment to cherish. I was feeling proud of my cousin and I realized that he was now a celebrated person of his school. After the match was over, I congratulated my cousin and told him that the entire sports event was a blast and I have enjoyed a lot by coming to the event and by watching the match.

CUE-CARD - 49 : MY FAVOURITE FOOD

- ★ What kind of food do you like?
- ★ How do you feel after eating it?
- ★ Do you know how to cook it?

My favourite food is the *Pakistani food* and my favourite dish is *Biryani*. I like to eat the Pakistani food because I have been eating it since my childhood and am fond of eating spicy food. I have been to many countries in this world and I have tried many things, but still I consider Pakistani food to be my favourite food. Some people like to eat things which are expensive and they feel that the things which they eat or like are recognized worldwide, but I have a different opinion. I like to eat things which are delicious and the food which I have been eating since my childhood.

I remember that once I was feeling very sad, and I did not want to eat anything at all. But then as I saw Biryani and I began feeling hungry. There are times when I am not even feeling hungry, and I start eating Biryani the moment I look at it. I feel very good after eating Biryani. It is so mouth-watering and sumptuous that sometimes I eat it in high quantities.

Some people think that only girls should be the ones who cook, but I think, boys should also know how to cook food. I learnt making this dish and it was a unique kind of experience. I never thought that cooking was so fun, and now whenever I want to eat Biryani, I prefer to make it myself. I believe that you should also try it out someday as most people in my country love it so much.

CUE-CARD - 50 : MY FAVOURITE DRINK

- ★ Name of your favourite drink.
- ★ Tell me something about the taste.
- ★ When do you drink it.

My favourite drink is Mountain Dew. I drink it every day and you can say that I am almost addicted to it. I cannot live a day without it. My fridge is always stuffed with chilled cans of Mountain Dew. It was 5 years ago when I saw the ad of Mountain Dew. I was really impressed by the adventurous ad of Mountain Dew and thought of trying it out. The surprising thing is that I liked it the first time, I tasted it and the entire feeling was incredible.

It is easy to tell about the taste of the drink. It has a unique taste and it feels as if there is lemon in the drink. The drink tastes the best when it is chilled. I cannot describe the feeling and taste, but you could get a good idea of its quality and taste, if you try it yourself.

I drink it every day. This is the reason why I have been putting on a lot of weight. Mountain dew has a lot of calories, but I just ignore the calories as I am a slave to its taste. I drink 1500-ml bottle everyday and I prefer to drink this while I am having dinner. I do not get angry at people and it is very difficult to annoy me but once, I had put my Mountain Dew in the fridge, and my cousin drank. This thing irritated me so much that I shouted at him. I am just so possessive about mountain dew that I cannot tolerate anyone else drinking my drink and getting all the pleasures.

CUE-CARD - 51 : MY FAVOURITE WEBSITE

- ★ Why is it your favourite website?
- ★ How often do you use it?
- ★ What would your life be without it?

My favourite website is *youtube.com.* A lot of people in this world regard *youtube* to be their favourite website and I feel in the similar way. This is a website in which a person can watch or upload videos for free, and the best part is that the user can even create his or her channel and then earn money by the videos he or she has uploaded. We can find almost everything on youtube and everything is available over there free of charge.

I started using youtube 4 years ago and it has been really a great experience. I spend most of my lesiure time on youtube. I have uploaded my own video lectures on youtube and these video lectures are provided to people for free. I also stay on youtube to watch trailers and songs. You can find almost every song of this world on youtube. There was a day when I missed a cricket match because I was busy in something, but because of youtube I was able to watch the entire match again because someone had uploaded the match and it made me very happy.

My life would be hell without youtube. I would not be able to function without it. I am running an educational institute in Pakistan, and I provide free online video lectures to everyone irrespective of the fact that they are my students or not. If youtube goes out of my life, I would not be able to provide this free service and it would be bad not only for me, but also for all the people who are benefitting from it.

CUE-CARD - 52 : IMPORTANCE OF EXERCISE

- ★ When do you exercise?
- ★ What exercise do you do?
- ★ How do you feel after doing exercise?

I do not think that anyone in this world can deny the importance of exercise in their life. I have seen that people who do exercise live a healthy and wealthy life. I would even consider obesity as a disease which deserves to be eradicated from this world.

I definitely know about the signifiance of exercise because at first, I used to be very fat. I weighed 200 pounds and I was obsessed with junk food. I got so much fat that I started hating myself. One day, I made a commitment to myself that I would lose my weight and that could only be done through exercise.

I started off with jogging on the treadmill, but as time progressed, I also began weight training. The exercise which I like the most is running or jogging. After jogging, I feel as if I am flying high up in the air and I feel very good. I run for about 30 minutes every day and it is a very good experience. Last month, I had to go out of town for a business meeting. As I was attending the meeting I did not get a chance to do my regular exercise and felt so bad. Some people say that they feel tired after doing exercise, but that is not the case with me. Whenever I do exercise, I feel energetic and am able to perform my other tasks in a better manner. I would recommend everyone to indulge in some kind of exercise because it would make a person both mentally and physically fit.

MOST POPULAR DISCUSSION TOPICS

The topic of discussion is related to the topics of the second part (a Speech/Cue card), but the difference is that here you should EXPRESS AN OPINION and explain why it is and what it is. This is the part where you should compare two opinions, present several points of view, say what your perception is, what future developments might follow, etc.

This part usually takes 4-5 minutes.

It's difficult to predict exactly what questions will be asked in the third part of the exam, but usually they will have a close connection to the topics we discussed in Part 2 of the exam. In addition, the following functions may be tested:

1. Comparing (time/objects/concepts)
2. Predicting
3. Advantages
4. Disadvantages
5. Problems
6. Solutions
7. Opinions (why)

1. Comparing

Do you think people were smarter in the past?

What is the difference between learning skills and knowledge?

2. Predicting

Do you think people will be more intelligent in the future?

Do you think technology can replace teachers in the future?

3. Advantages

What are the main advantages of studying online?

What are the main advantages of studying abroad?

4. **Disadvantages**

What are the main disadvantages of studying online?

What are the main disadvantages of studying abroad?

5. **Problems**

What are some of the main problems that students often encounter while learning English?

What problems do students often have with their classmates?

6. **Solutions**

[for above "how could we solve these problems"]

7. **Opinion**

Why do you think some people enjoy learning new things?

What are some useful ways to remember things?

1. **Comparing:** Try to use the language of comparison (cheaper, more expensive, more/ less than)

   Opening: Well, obviously, there are a variety of possible differences here; Well, undoubtedly, they are like chalk and cheese.

   The First Difference: However, I (guess/ suppose) that the most striking difference is ~; whereas in contrast… But I would say the most fundamental would be that (S+V). On the contrary,

   The Second Difference: In addition, a subsequent contrast could be that (S+V). Conversely, moreover, a further distinction might be that (S+V). While on the other hand, ...

Practice Questions for Part 3 of the IELTS EXAM

- ★ In what ways do the magazines are different from newspapers?
- ★ How could we deal with the problems of Internet?
- ★ Are people travelling more now than in the past?
- ★ Who make better teachers – men or women?
- ★ How have family values changed over the years?

2. **Predicting:** Try to use future tense (will, going to + verb)

   Opening: I am sure that in years to come, we will see a number of changes related to this; I imagine that in the near future, we will witness some major changes with regards to (N).

The First Prediction: To begin with, I would predict that we will most likely to have (N). Primarily, it looks quite possible that we are going to have (N).

The Second Prediction: As well as, some people claim that we will probably start to see (N). Likewise, I would imagine that we may even be able to see (N).

The Third Prediction: And who knows, there is even a chance that we will have (N). And I know it is a bit of a crazy thought, but one day we may even have (N).

Practice Questions for Part 3 of the IELTS EXAM

- ✯ What will schools be like in the future?
- ✯ What will cars be like in the future?
- ✯ Do you think people will have to conserve water in the future?
- ✯ Do you think we will get the news in different ways in the future?
- ✯ What will your country be like in 50 years?

3. **Advantages (merits, benefits, rewards)**

Opening: Clearly there are a number of obvious merits; Obviously there are a number of positive features.

The Main Advantage: But I would probably say that for the most part, the one thing that really stands out is that~. This is obviously favourable because (S+V). However, I guess that the most evident would be that (S+V). This is surely a positive feature as (S+V).

The Second Advantage: Besides this, a second plus point could be that (S+V). This is undoubtedly favourable and at the same time, a second bonus might be that of (S+V).

Practice Questions for Part 3 of the IELTS EXAM

- ✯ What are the advantages of living in an old building?
- ✯ What are the advantages of living in big cities?
- ✯ What are the advantages of owning an up-to-date mobile phone?
- ✯ What are the advantages of advertising?
- ✯ What are the advantages of studying abroad?

4. **Disadvantages (drawbacks, shortcomings)**

Opening: I am sure most people would agree that there are some drawbacks; Of course, there are a couple of shortcomings.

The Main Disadvantage: I suppose the most unfavourable quality might be that (S+V). This is a weakness obviously because of (S+V). I guess the most impractical characteristic would be that of (S+V). This is a clear limitation because of (S+V).

The Second Disadvantage: At the same time, another stumbling block might be that ~. And the trouble with this is that... Correspondingly, an additional weak point may be that (S+V). And this can be a hassle as~...

Practice Questions for Part 3 of the IELTS EXAM

- ✯ What are the disadvantages of living in an old building?
- ✯ What are the disadvantages of living in big cities?
- ✯ What are the disadvantages of owning an up-to-date mobile phone?
- ✯ What are the disadvantages of advertising?
- ✯ What are the disadvantages of studying abroad?

5. **Problems**

Opening: Obviously, we can say that there are quite a lot of dangers with regard to this issue. It is universally accepted that there are a few hazards involved with (N).

The Main Problem: Essentially, one fundamental concern is probably that ~. This is clearly alarming because~.

The Second Problem: Equally worrying is the suggestion that~. And the underlying repercussions of this are...

Practice Questions for Part 3 of the IELTS EXAM

- ✯ What problems are associated with eating fast food?
- ✯ What problems are caused by a lack of physical exercise?
- ✯ How is our busy lifestyle contributing to health problems?
- ✯ What problems are associated with global warming?
- ✯ What problems are associated with violence being shown on TV?

6. **Solutions:**

Opening: In my view, there are a few ways to tackle this problem.

The First Solution: When dealing with __________, the easiest way to solve it out would be ~.

The Second Solution: I also think that we could ________________

Practice Questions for Part 3 of the IELTS EXAM

- ✯ How could we deal with eating fast food?
- ✯ What would you do to get more physical exercise?
- ✯ How can stress from our busy lifestyle be relieved?
- ✯ What steps could be taken to tackle global warming?
- ✯ How could kids be prevented from seeing violence on TV?

7. **Opinion (why)**

Opening: Well in my opinion, there are undoubtedly a variety of justifications for this. I suppose I would say that (S+V). There are probably a number of factors involved. Well generally, it is my belief that (S+V). There are obviously a number of motives surrounding this idea.

The First Reason: The chief cause might be that (S+V). The key explanation is possibly because of (S+V).

The Second Reason: As well as this, a subsequent factor could be because of (S+V). At the same time, a secondary motive could be that of (S+V).

Practice Questions for Part 3 of the IELTS EXAM

- ✯ Why do people like travelling to foreign countries?
- ✯ Why do so many people move from the countryside to cities?
- ✯ Why is it important for children to play sports?
- ✯ Why do young people spend so much time on the Internet?
- ✯ Why is watching TV so popular all over the world?

POPULAR DISCUSSION TOPICS

GIFTS

1. What are the positive/negative aspects of giving and receiving gifts?

Ans: Giving and receiving gifts have both advantages and disadvantages. On one hand, it is an expression of one's love or appreciation for someone, and on the other hand, it strengthens relationships. It can also create a good feeling in the minds of people.

On the other hand, giving and receiving gifts today has become a commercial activity. Sometimes we are forced to give and receive gifts. A lot of time and money are involved in buying gifts. For example, if someone calls you for a birthday, you are compelled to give a gift. Sometimes, it can become a burden on your budget.

2. What are the different types of gifts that women, men and children would like to receive?

Ans: Women are usually fond of ornaments and clothes. They also like to receive household appliances and handicrafts. For special occasions, like birthdays, they receive a lot of such gifts. Children are usually attracted to toys and dolls. They love chocolates and sweets too.

3. What changes have taken place in giving and receiving gifts in the last 50 years?

Ans: A number of changes have taken place in the way people give and receive gifts, over the last 50 years. In the olden days, gifts were not very common and it was exchanged only during rare occasions like marriages. Today, giving and receiving gifts have become a very frequent affair. Exchanging gifts have become very common on a number of occasions like birthdays, anniversaries and success in an exam.

4. Whose gifts do you treasure most?

Ans: I treasure the gifts of my loved ones. For instance, I always cherish the gifts that my wife has given me. In fact, she gives them to me with great love. I greatly value gifts from my parents too. Gifts from close friends or colleagues also give me great pleasure.

5. Do you think people have become more or less materialistic in the last 25 years?

Ans: What I feel is, people's attitude towards material things have not changed over the last 25 years. The only difference is that today we have greater access to comforts and luxuries unlike in the past, and we have enough money to buy them, so we enjoy them. For this reason, many people tend to say that materialism is on the increase. Actually, that is not the case. If people in the past had access to such things and if they had as much money as we have today, they would have definitely enjoyed luxuries. The only difference is the economic progress that we have made. The attitude towards materialism remains the same always.

I feel that people have definitely become more materialistic during the last 25 years. Formerly, comforts and luxuries were not available to people as much as we have today. Maybe, people were more idealistic and they had better human relationships. Especially in rural communities, people maintained traditional values in families and social life. Whereas, today the situation has changed. Urbanisation has forced people to be more individualistic and achievement-oriented. Material achievement has become a major purpose in life and therefore, I think, other values of life have taken a back seat.

6. What kind of gifts children usually like?

Ans: Children usually like chocolates, toys and electronic games. You know, for example, if you go to a shop with your children, you will see them running to the toy corner or the chocolate rack. These days, a lot of children have a great liking towards electronic games. There are many children who like cartoons and story books too.

7. What kind of things give a sense of prestige to people today?

Ans: From my personal experience, I feel, material possessions can give a great deal of prestige to people today. For example, if you have a luxurious car or a beautifully designed house it can give you a sense of pride. Another important criterion for prestige is political power at different levels, which can make you popular and accepted by the society. Superior positions in government services can also definitely give you prominence in the society. What I mean is, senior police officers, judges and similar officials have great prestige in the society. Apart from that, superior education can give you a lot of honour among the people. Certain professionals like doctors, engineers and teachers are respected in the society.

8. What kind of things were status symbols in your grandfather's time?

Ans: Although I am not very sure, money and other material possessions were status symbols even in my grandparents' time. I think, people who had a lot of land were considered honourable in the society. Superior education and political power were also considered status symbols at that time. I believe, basically, the status symbols of people of all ages are generally the same.

9. What kind of things are women usually attracted to?

Ans: Women are generally fond of good clothes and ornaments. If you go to a textile store or jewellery shop, the majority of the shoppers are usually women. This means that there is a certain vanity in women and they love to flaunt their beauty. They are also attracted to cosmetics. Many women buy a lot of house hold appliances and crockery.

10. **Do you think people purchase a lot of things for prestige and not because of genuine need?**

Ans: Certainly, today if you have money to spare, you certainly buy things that can show off your wealth. Although you may not need such luxurious items, you buy them because you want others to look upon you. For example, one of the considerations for many people, when they choose a car, is whether a particular car is used by the elite in the society. Or, even if the family is a small one, people build huge houses and many of the rooms are unused for years. Prestige is a serious consideration for many people these days.

11. **What will be the kind of things that will give a sense of prestige to people in future?**

Ans: Even in the future, wealth will be a major determining factor which is a sense of prestige to people. Education, the expertise in technology and communication abilities also give a sense of pride to the people.

FAMILY

1. **In what ways can people in a family be similar to each other?**

Ans: People in a family can be similar to each other in many ways. They usually resemble each other in their physical appearances. For example, children look like their parents, in their facial features, colour, type of hair and so on. They can also be alike, in their character and behaviour.

2. **Do you think daughters are always more similar to mothers than to the other male relatives?**

Ans: Not always! There are many daughters who look more like their fathers or other male members of the family than mothers. That includes their colour, face, hair and so on. But I do think that most daughters look like their mothers in physical features.

3. **What about sons and fathers?**

Ans: I think it is the same with them as well. There are many sons who resemble their mothers more than their fathers or other male members of the family.

4. **In terms of personality, are people more influenced by their family or friends? In what ways?**

Ans: People are usually more influenced by their family than friends, because as children, most people live with their families. And that is when an individual's personality is developed. Even after that, people spend more time with their family members and interact with them more closely than their friends. This intimacy with the family members has a great influence in their character formation. On the other hand, friends also have a significant influence on one's personality, but not as much as family members.

GENETIC RESEARCH

1. Where can people in your country get information about genetic research?

Ans: There are many sources in my country where people can get information about genetic research. I think the most common source is a book. You can find books on genetic research in public libraries or in bookshops. Apart from that, there are a number of universities and institutes that do research in genetic studies. There are lots of scientists and professors who can give information about this subject. I think the internet is a wonderful source to get information about genetic research. If you search on Google, you will come across many websites that will give you, at least, the primary information about genetic research.

2. How do people in your country feel about genetic research?

Ans: In general, I think people in my country have a positive attitude towards genetic research. They know it has a lot of benefits in terms of better agricultural production and prevention of many genetic diseases. However, some people are worried about genetically modified foods. They fear that it can be dangerous to human health.

3. Should this research be funded by the governments or private companies?

Ans: I think both government and private companies should jointly or separately fund genetic research. It should not be the monopoly of either of the parties. If private companies alone fund genetic research, the benefits of the research may not reach the common man, because of their profit motive. So the government also has the responsibility to fund it, so that everybody enjoys the benefits.

TRAFFIC WHERE YOU LIVE

1. How do most people travel to work where you live?

Ans: Most people in my place travel to work using the public transport system. We have both government and private bus services that are very efficient and frequent. The bus fares are also quiet moderate, and that makes it the favourite mode of travel for ordinary people to go to work. People, who go to longer distances to work, usually make use of trains. We have a number of short distance trains, which are very inexpensive. A lot of people also have their own private vehicles to go to work. Most young people have their own motorbikes. The more affluent go to work by car.

2. What traffic problems are there in your area?

Ans: Traffic problems are quite frequent in my area, especially during the peak hours of morning and evening, when people travel to work or study and come back. Many roads are very narrow and cannot hold the increasing traffic volume at a time. So traffic moves at a snail's pace, especially during the rush hours. There are also a lot of puddles on the roads, particularly during the rainy season and manoeuvring them would further slow the traffic down. There are constant repairs on the roads which are both slow and ineffective and traffic is often diverted through narrower roads making the situation still worse.

3. **How do traffic problems affect you?**

Ans: Traffic problems affect me very badly. I need to reach work on time and very often, the unexpected traffic snarls and jams do not let me do it. I have made it a point that I start a bit earlier from home, so that these unexpected delays do not affect me much. Another problem is that driving in high gear in the traffic jam exhausts my fuel tank very fast.

4. **How would you reduce the traffic problems in your area?**

Ans: The first thing that the government should do is to widen the roads with immediate effect and that can definitely reduce the problems drastically. Another area that the authorities can look into is to engage a big company to construct roads that can last for a longer period of time. It would definitely reduce the constant repairs on roads. People should also be made to obey traffic rules very strictly.

PARTY

1. **What types of parties do people have, and why are parties important?**

Ans: People have parties to celebrate special occasions like birthdays, weddings, or the beginning of a new year. I think it's important to celebrate these things because they are landmarks in our lives. Parties are a good way to bring people together, and they're an opportunity to let off some steam.

2. **Why do you think some people like parties but others hate them?**

Ans: Most people like parties because they have a good time at them – eating a nice meal, chatting to friends, or dancing. People who don't like them might find social situations difficult because they are shy, or maybe, they don't enjoy making small talk with people they don't know.

3. **Do you think parties will become more popular in the future?**

Ans: No, I don't think anything will change. People have always had parties, and I'm sure they always will in the future. Humans need to socialise and enjoy themselves, and parties are one of the best ways to do that.

DECISION

1. **Is it better to make important life decisions on your own or is it better to consult other people?**

Ans: There are good reasons for both, I suppose. Ultimately, it's your life so I suppose you should make the decisions. On the other hand, any decisions you make can affect other people, so it seems only right to discuss things with others first. Like many philosophical questions, there's no simple answer, I'm afraid.

2. **Do you think good decision-making can be taught?**

Ans: Well, if you go to a bookstore, you'll see lots of self-help books that claim to teach decision-making. I'm not sure any of them are effective though. I suppose it depends on the type of decision you mean. If it's a business strategy, then I'm sure some decisions are better than others and business schools teach this. But if it's a moral issue then I'm not sure anyone can claim to know the right decision, so how can anyone teach it?

LEISURE TIME

1. **Is watching TV a good way of forgetting about work or study?**

Ans: Absolutely, yes. These days there's so much choice available that we can completely immerse ourselves in entertainment. I mean, you can turn on a good drama or comedy show and pretty soon, you forget about everything that happened that day. I think that without TV we'd all go a little crazy.

2. **Should coworkers also spend their leisure time together?**

Ans: I'm completely against this. The problem with people going out together after work is that they just gossip about certain people in the office or factory, and this can hardly be a good thing for the company, can it? Another thing is that there's always the risk that you will say something you regret after a few drinks and then you have to face your colleagues again the next day. So, in short, I would definitely advise people to think twice about socialising with colleagues.

TOURISM

1. **What do you think are the preferred places for tourism in your country?**

Ans. My country, India is a tourist paradise. We have all sorts of destination for people of varied tastes. From Kashmir to Kanayakumari, India is blend with natural beauty, ethnic splendour and cultural diversity in the form of hill stations like Mussorie, Dalhousie, Shimla, Ooty, etc. The natural paradise on earth is KASHMIR.

2. **What are the negative impacts of tourism?**

Ans. Well, I've seen areas where large number of visitors have had a detrimental effect on local habitats. Excessive use of natural resources, danger of epidemics and excise or imports issues including threats of terrorism can't be ignored.

3. **How do you think can we make tourism better for the local community?**

Ans. Undoubtedly, the local economy really uproars if the tourism is promoted in a better way. It does not only increase the Gross Domestic Product (GDP) of the place but rather, it adds value to the national Exchange. But the need of the hour is to preserve and protect it.

4. **How has tourism changed in your country over the last 10 years?**

Ans. Tourism has changed manifold. Tourism brings investment and better infrastructure to poorer communities. It brings the improved quality of life for the local people. It also brings greater work opportunities for the local people. For example, earlier they are limited to fishing and farming but nowdays, it offers high earning jobs.

5. **How do you think will it change in the future?**

Ans. Well..I must say in the coming years, our economic development largely depends upon the tourism sector. It will strengthen universal brotherhood, fraternity, international world peace and exchange of cultural values.

6. **How well equipped is your country to deal with tourists?**

Ans. Ahhh…Very interesting, but I must say presently, we are under the grip of loopholes as most of the tourist centres like Taj Mahal…the Seven Wonders of the World, are facing a severe threat of pollution. Similarly, wildlife sanctuaries are also facing the problem of *extinction, poaching and hunting*. Historical sites are losing their charms due to faster means of globalisation and communication. So catering interest among tourists for visiting these places seems to be a hard nut to crack.

EDUCATION

1. **What do you think are important skills for a teacher?**

Ans. A teacher is the milestone that plays an indispensable role in building up of a nation. For a student is a mirror where the transparent picture of a subject can be easily seen. So it is quite essential that the teacher should be well educated, cultured, disciplined, most important is up-to-date with the present scenario in his/her subject of teaching. Here I must say, he/she should be an *Encyclopaedia of knowledge*.

2. **What facilities should a school have?**

Ans. Giving and getting Smart Education is the order of the day. Gone are those days when teachers were restricted to chalk and blackboard. Today in this smarter world, the teacher and student both need to be smarter to get the best and practical education. Each and every school should try to facilitate the system of *Smart Education* in the form of *Online Education.*

3. **What are the problems with the education system in your country?**

Ans: Education is the gateway to success. But if steps are not proper, it may lead to ignorance and darkness. Our education system is also in the grip of a number of problems like Utopian Education (Imaginary), more stress on examination rather than putting efforts for building up of attitude and aptitude in knowledge. Undoubtedly, it is flexible and experimental these days but sometimes, it is all Greek to those who are unable to answer it.

4. **What can be done to solve these problems?**

Ans. More stress should be laid down upon Smart and Practical Education to improve its standards. *Time Immemorial Syllabus* should be immediately banned, i.e., the quality of curriculum should be changed according to the the times, so that students become more updated to the present scenario.

5. **What do you think the typical classroom will look like in 20 years?**

Ans.The typical chalk-blackboard classroom will be converted into high profile online classrooms where the creation and proliferation of the personal computer, the globalization of ideas and other human acts, and the use of technology in exchanging ideas and providing access to more people will be done.

SKILLS

1. **How important is it to have a skill?**

Ans. Keeping and having skills are the indispensable requirement in the vocational, professional and occupational world. Gone are those days when degrees or diplomas are sufficient to get any job but these days, it is necessary to possess skills like language, communication, IT, man power, techniques, etc.These skills are even highly lucrative as far as monetary aspect is concerned.

2. **What is the most useful skill you have?**

Ans. Well ..I do believe possessing skills is the inherent requirement of the present scenario. The most useful skill what I have is that of Communication. I do believe that this skill is the need of the hour as the world is governed according to this skill. Possessing good command over language not only enhances your language skills, but also allows you to interact with the world.

3. **How can children learn different skills?**

Ans. Children are the nation builders of tomorrow. It is highly essential for them to possess skills like communication, IT, techniques, dance, acting, swimming, etc. They can learn these skills while doing their academic education in school. Moreover, it is the moral responsibility of the schools to open avenues for children to adhere to these skills, so that they should not academically be brilliant but also talented and skilled in the art of doing some practical work.

4. Can anyone be a good artist/singer, etc.?

Ans. Yes..of course, why not. I know talent and skill both are different terms but if we try to polish the talent, then it becomes a good skill that helps anybody to achieve higher in life. For example, anybody can be a good artist or singer if he/she is learned and practised in a right way because possessing talent is not sufficient enough until or unless it is polished to form a skill.

THE ENVIRONMENT

1. How can we teach people to care more about the environment?

Ans. Undoubtedly, it is the next generation who will have to bear the burden of saving the planet. So it is necessary to alert them with the havoc of environmental problems like Global Warming, Depletion of Natural Resources, Scarcity of Water, Pollution, etc. For this, they should be given proper statistics and survey details of all these problems so that the coming generation should understand its urgency and take proper repercussions to improve the environmental problems.

2. Are people in your country aware of environmental problems?

Ans. To be honest, no... I think the middle and upper classes are mad in the rat race of earning and spending money, and there are many people in my country, who live below the poverty line and they quite literally can't afford to worry about the environment when they are struggling to put food on the table and just survive.

3. What is the biggest environmental issue in your country at the moment?

Ans. Global warming is the major issue in my country at the moment because it results not only in the depletion of the ozone layer but also responsible for creating suffocation and congestion in the environment.

4. Does the responsibility for protecting the environment lie with the governments or with the individuals?

Ans. In my view, the responsibility lies with all of us. However, individuals, at least in my country, aren't taking action of their own accord and nor our businesses, they are just out to make profits. The government also fails to force people to be more green, for example by fining companies or factory owners that release toxic waste into our rivers or incentivising us to recycle.

BOOKS

1. How important are books to you?

Ans. Books are my best friends which never demand and never complain. It is the *Store house of Knowledge*. It directs us towards our goals. It also improves our Focus and Vision towards Life.

2. Do you think that children don't read enough these days?

Ans. Yes..certainly in the world of e-books, reading habits are dashed into the ground in the children's world. They love to do Net Surfing instead of getting engrossed into the bookish world. But those who are fond of reading still love reading novels at length.

3. How can we make sure that children should keep reading?

Ans. Well, here I must say children of present day are more observatory and experimental rather than theoretical.We can make sure children should keep reading by using the art of creativity to cater their interests because reading simple text without graphics seems to be cumbersome and a hard nut to crack for them. So it is better to have animated, creative and fantasy based books to maintain their art of reading.

4. What impact has new technology on books and reading?

Ans. New technology brings revolutionary change on books and reading. It brings the era of e-books. Nowdays, with the mushroom growth of science and technology, media, television channels, etc., its scope becomes more widened and broad. Now online oriented material takes the place of manual text.

5. How do book preferences now compared to preferences in the past?

Ans. Well, earlier people were fond of reading Religious Books.They were more inclined to books related to philosophy. But today in the era of E-books, students are more aware of experimental knowledge. They become more factual than value based.

6. Do you think in the future paper books will disappear all together?

Ans. Certainly..Here I must say not in future, rather even in the present education system too, the era of smart books has invaded the global education system. It has replaced paper books to great extent. Even the school infrastructure is designed on behalf of giving smarter education to children for this purpose. Smart screens are used for providing online education in place of chalk Blackboard pedagogy .

TECHNOLOGY

1. Do you like the new technology/gadgets?

Ans. Yes… why not ..of course..it is the order of the day. Without it life is indispensable. I love the gadgetary world and its equipments as it makes life more comfortable and pleasant to live. It removes the definition of isolation from the world and allows the networking of social sites which brings revolutionary change in the culture of socialisation.

2. How important is technology in your life?

Ans. To be very frank, I must say life will be burdensome if technology is not in my life. It is one of the cheapest and best source to lead a comfortable life. It has excelled the field beyond one's expectations. Whatever area it may be, whether it is medical, communication, insurance, education, science, etc..it leaves its blueprint remarkably.

3. Which device has had the biggest impact on daily life?

Undoubtedly, the Internet has the biggest impact on our daily lives. It is the revolutionary invention of the 21st century. With the advent of internet, the world has been converted in to a global village. It is the house of information, door of social networking sites, education package for youngsters, package of games and leisure time activities for children.

4. How does communication these days differ from communication 10 years ago?

Ans. Well, earlier communication took place in the form of postal letters and telephonic conversation, but these days, the mode of communication has completely changed. E-mails, the fastest mode of transportation, has excelled the field of communication beyond one's expectations. Earlier television was the only media of knowing information. Nowdays, in the era of gadgetary world, mobile devices like cellular phones, tablets, I-pads, etc. have improved the modes of communication.

5. What are the disadvantages of all this technology?

Ans. We are becoming the servants in thought, as in action, of the machine we have created to serve us. Technology... is a queer thing. It brings you great gifts with one hand, and it stabs you at the back with the other. It makes your life more lethargic. It offers a sedentary life style where there is no physical exercise of the body.

LEARNING A LANGUAGE

1. How hard do you find it to learn a language?

Ans. Yes, it is true. Sometimes, its tough to learn the phonetics of alphabets of the second language, as it is not our mother tongue. So the best way to understand the second language is to meet the same folk of people belonging to that language for regular communication and only exchange of words in the same language enchances your language capacities. Learning the English language for the first time can be difficult. However, when done in an exciting and humorous way, learning English vocabulary and grammar are less confusing and more enjoyable.

2. **What aspects do you find the most difficult?**

Ans. Language is the medium of communication. If the individual excelled in the art of speaking a language, then it understands how to communicate in the same language with, other people. So I think communication in the same language is the most difficult aspect.

3. **Is it necessary to learn the culture of a country to understand its language?**

Ans. Every language is a temple, in which the soul of those who speak it is enshrined. *Language is the mirror of every culture.* The way we communicate becomes our caste, colour and creed. As you know, I belong to India which is a multilingual state, with unity in diversity, so language becomes the most significant factor that distinguishes one culture from other which later united us into one nation. For example, Punjabi belongs to Punjab people, Marathi belongs to Maharashtra the but together, we are only Indian. So I think, one can easily learn about the culture of a country by the way we communicate.

4. **Is it possible to get a good job these days without knowing a second language?**

Well.... these days .., I must say... no...It is tough for Indians to get a job on behalf of their mother tongue. As we are living in the environment of MNCs and corporates which work with English based nations requires employees who know English to communicate their business. So undoubtedly, it is very hard to survive on mother tongue alone these days.

5. **How can people best learn a language?**

The best way to learn any language is to communicate with those people who are using that language as their means of communication. The other ways to learn a foreign language is to watch movies in that language, listen to audio Cds /Dvd's of the language you wish to learn.

ABSTRACT

LISTENING MODULE

In listening module we endeavour to help the candidate to know the pointers, tips and common errors in listening section and for practice we enclose here with Three Listening Practice Tests for candidates.

Chapter 9 : Listening Strategies & Skills

LISTENING MODULE IELTS

Duration & Format:

- ✯ First Module IELTS test of 30 minutes
- ✯ Test is played once only
- ✯ Approximately 30 minutes + 10 minutes transfer time
- ✯ Total 40 Questions

STRUCTURE OF THE TEST

	No. of Speakers	No. of items (Questions)
Section One	Conversation between two speakers	Ten (10)
Section Two	One Speaker	Ten (10)
Section Three	Conversation between two & four speakers	Ten (10)
Section Four	One speaker	Ten (10)

Question Types

- ✯ Short Answer Type
- ✯ Multiple Choice
- ✯ Matching
- ✯ Classification
- ✯ Summary Completion
- ✯ Sentence Completion
- ✯ Diagram Completion
- ✯ Table Completion
- ✯ Form Completion

Factors in The Assessment

- ✯ Proper understanding of foreign accent
- ✯ Recognize the role of speakers
- ✯ Understand and identifying numbers, dates and names
- ✯ Understand the general meaning of the conversation

TEST TIPS FOR LISTENING TEST

TIP NO. 1: ENCIRCLE THE KEY WORDS

In the beginning of the test, 40-45 seconds are alloted to candidate.During that time try to encircle the key words of listening sections.

TIP NO. 2: BE CAREFUL OF "W" Family

Focus what type of questions the speaker is talking about, i.e. What, Where When, Why, Whom.

TIP NO. 3: DONOT REPEAT THE INFORMATION

Do not rewrite the word which is already written in the question paer.

TIP NO. 4: LISTEN TO INSTRUCTIONS CAREFULLY

TIP NO. 5: NEVER CHECK YOUR ANSWERS

While attempting the test never check your answers, otherwise you will miss rest of the questions.

TIP NO. 6: QUERIES ARE IN CHRONOLOGICAL ORDER

TIP NO. 7: DO NOT EXCEED THE WORD LIMIT

Listening Practice Test 1

Section One

Listen to the journey of the 44th Black President of America 'BARACK OBAMA' and answer the following questions (1-7) on your answer sheet.

Circle the appropriate letter from (A-D).

1. Barack Obama took office on

A. 20th January, 2009

B. January 20, 2009

C. Jan 20, 2009

D. 2009, Jan 20

2. Barack Obama is the ____________________ of *Harvard Law Review.*

A. Attorney

B. President

C. African

D. Community Organizer

3. Barack Obama served the senate for three years as

A. Community Organizer

B. Civil Rights Attorney

C. President

D. Teacher

4. He was the Lecturer of ________________ in the University of Chicago Law School

A. Law

B. Constitution

C. Constitutional Law

D. None of these

5. **Barack Obama is not successful in the house of**

   A. U.S. Senate

   B. U.S. House of Representatives

   C. Democratic National Convention

   D. Harvard Law School

6. **Barack Obama RIVAL/Running Mate is**

   A. Joe Biden/Mc Cain

   B. Mc Cain/Delaware

   C. Mc Cain/Joe Biden

   D. Joe Biden

7. **Barack Obama won with**

   A. 70 % of votes

   B. 46 % of votes

   C. 53 % of votes

   D. None of these

BARACK OBAMA
PRESIDENT OF UNITED STATES

Section Two

Listen the profile of Barack Obama and answer the following questions (8-20) on your answer sheet.

- ✯ Born **8.** ______________________
- ✯ Youth Name **9.** ______________________
- ✯ Met Michelle Robinson, Wife in **10.** ______________________
- ✯ Married on **11.** ______________________ 1992
- ✯ First Daughter **12.** ______________________ in 1998
- ✯ SECOND DAUGHTER 'Sasha' in **13.** ______________________
- ✯ Family is just like **14.** ______________________
- ✯ Second Husband of Mother belongs to **15.** ______________________
- ✯ Favourite Sport **16.** ______________________
- ✯ Obama leave the habit of **17.** ______________________
- ✯ Religion **18.** ______________________
- ✯ Dreams from my father released in **19.** ______________________
- ✯ In 2007 he released **20.** ______________________

Section Three

Listen the description of an Umbrella by the narrator and answer the following questions from (21-28) on your answer sheet.

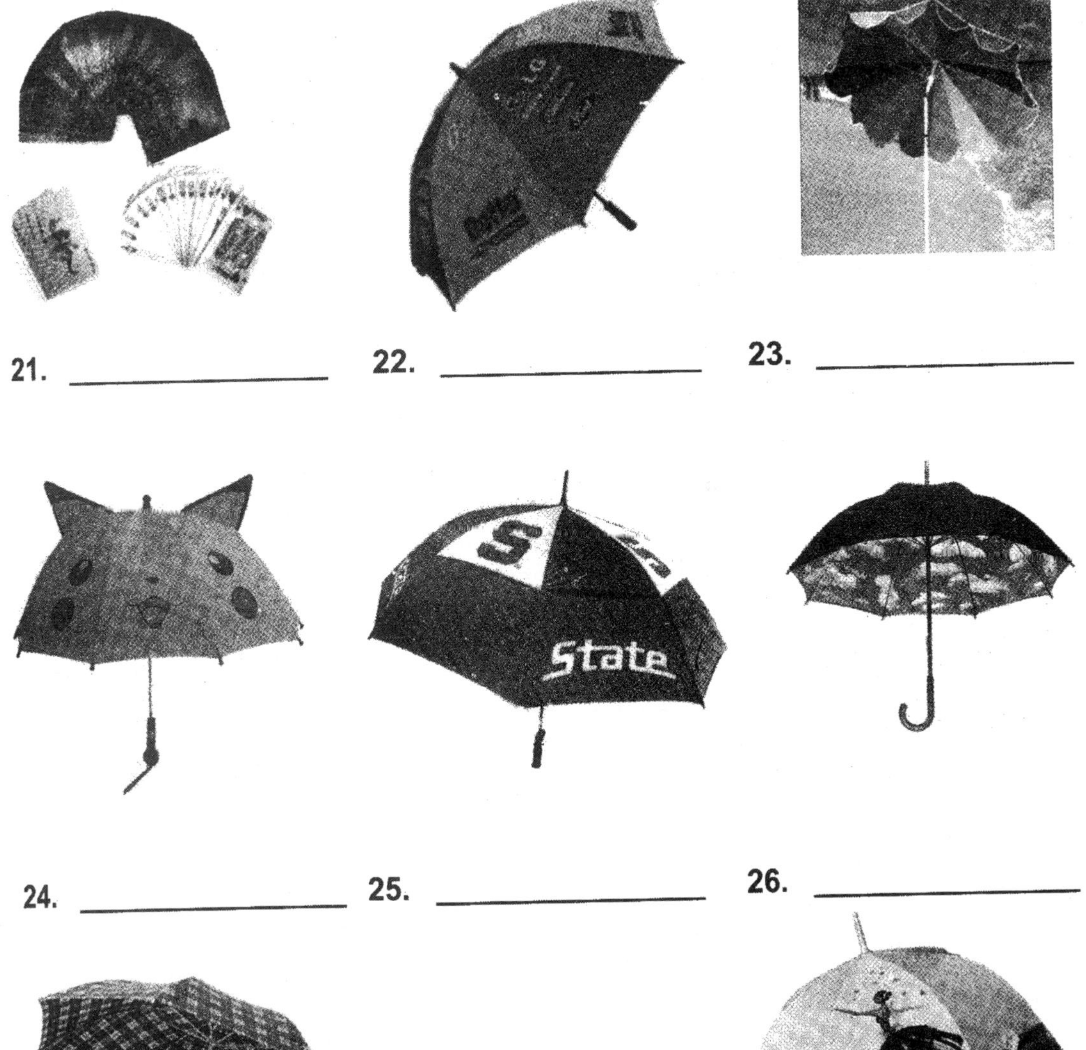

21. ________ 22. ________ 23. ________

24. ________ 25. ________ 26. ________

27. ________ 28. ________

Section Four

This section gives a brief idea of the courses offered for studying abroad in graduate and post-graduate classes in countries like, UK, Canada, Australia and New Zealand.

Listen the tapescript carefully and tick (✓) mark the following answer from (29-36) on your answer sheet.

Graduate Courses

	A	B	C	D	E	F	G
Country Name	Arts	Scinece	Business	Medicine	Commerce	Mathematics Science	Engineering
29. U.K.							
30. Canada							
31. Australia							
32. New Zealand							

Post Graduate Courses

Country Name	Medicine	Business	Arts	Social Sciences
33. U.K.	A	B	C	D
34. Canada				
35. Australia				
36. New Zealand				

Complete the following blanks:

37. PHD in Social Science offered in ____________________.

38. Canada offered ____________________ courses.

39. Australia offered PHD in ____________________ courses.

40. Degree/Diploma offered by ____________________.

Answer Sheet for Listening Test - 1

1.		**21.**	
2.		**22.**	
3.		**23.**	
4.		**24.**	
5.		**25.**	
6.		**26.**	
7.		**27.**	
8.		**28.**	
9.		**29.**	
10.		**30.**	
11.		**31.**	
12.		**32.**	
14.		**33.**	
15.		**34.**	
16.		**35.**	
17.		**36.**	
18.		**37.**	
19.		**39.**	
20.		**40.**	

Listening Total ________________

Listening Test 1

Answers

Section One

1. B	2. B	3. B	4. C
5. B	6. C	7. C	

Section Two

8. Aug, 4, 1961	9. Barry
10. June, 1989	11. October, 3
12. MaliaAnn	13. 2001
14. Mini United Nation	15. Indonesia
16. Basket Ball	17. Smoking
18. Christian	19. 1995
20. State of Black America	

Section Three

21. G	22. A	23. C	24. F
25. B	26. H	27. D	28. F

Section Four

29. B, D	30. E, F	31. A, B, C	32. A, B, E, F, G
33. A, B	34. C	35. B, C, D	36. B, D
37. UK	38. Vocational	39. Arts	40. New Zealand

Listening Practice Test – 2

Section One

Listen and tick (✓) A, B, C or D to indicate which picture in (1 – 8) questions is being discussed.

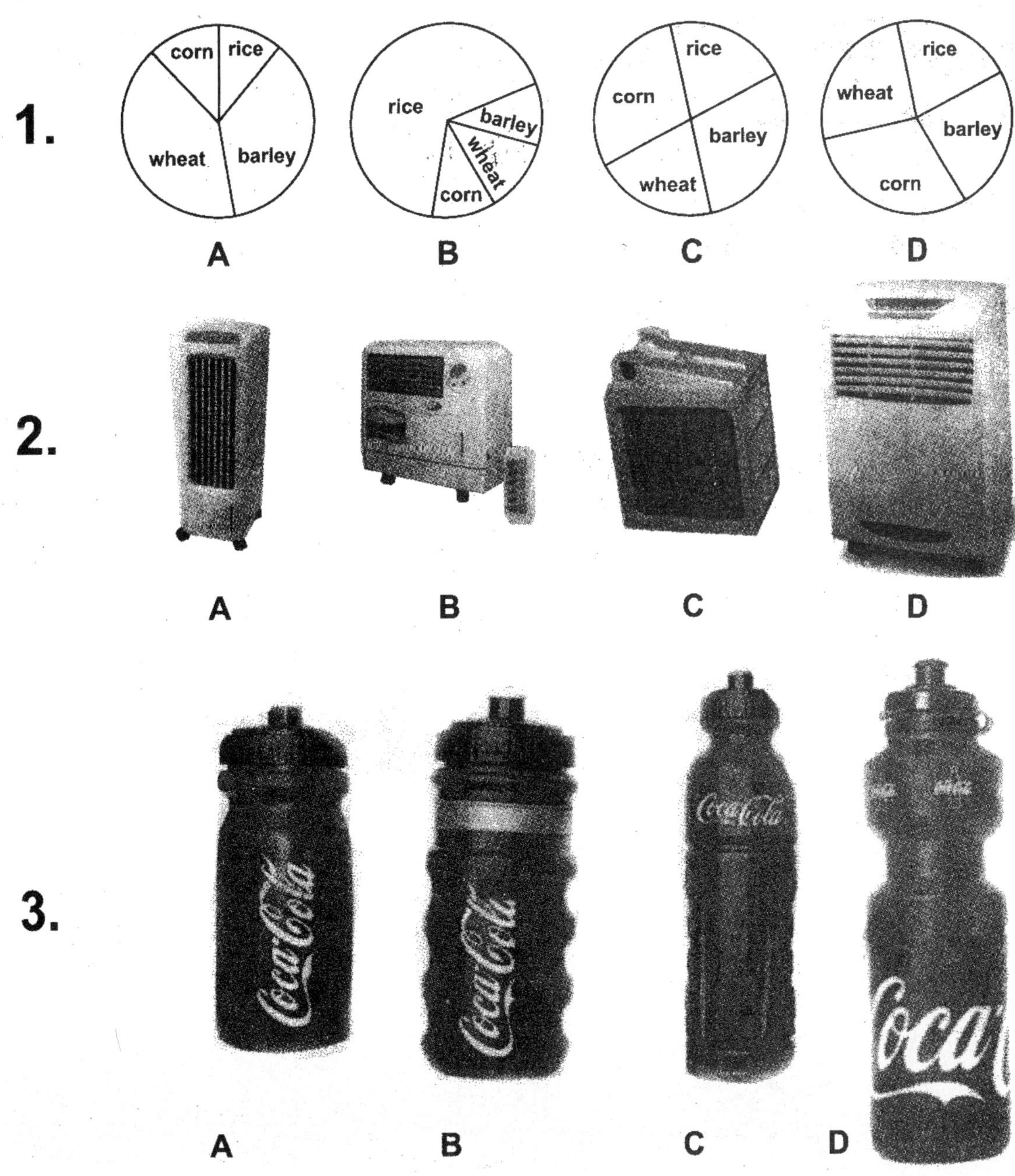

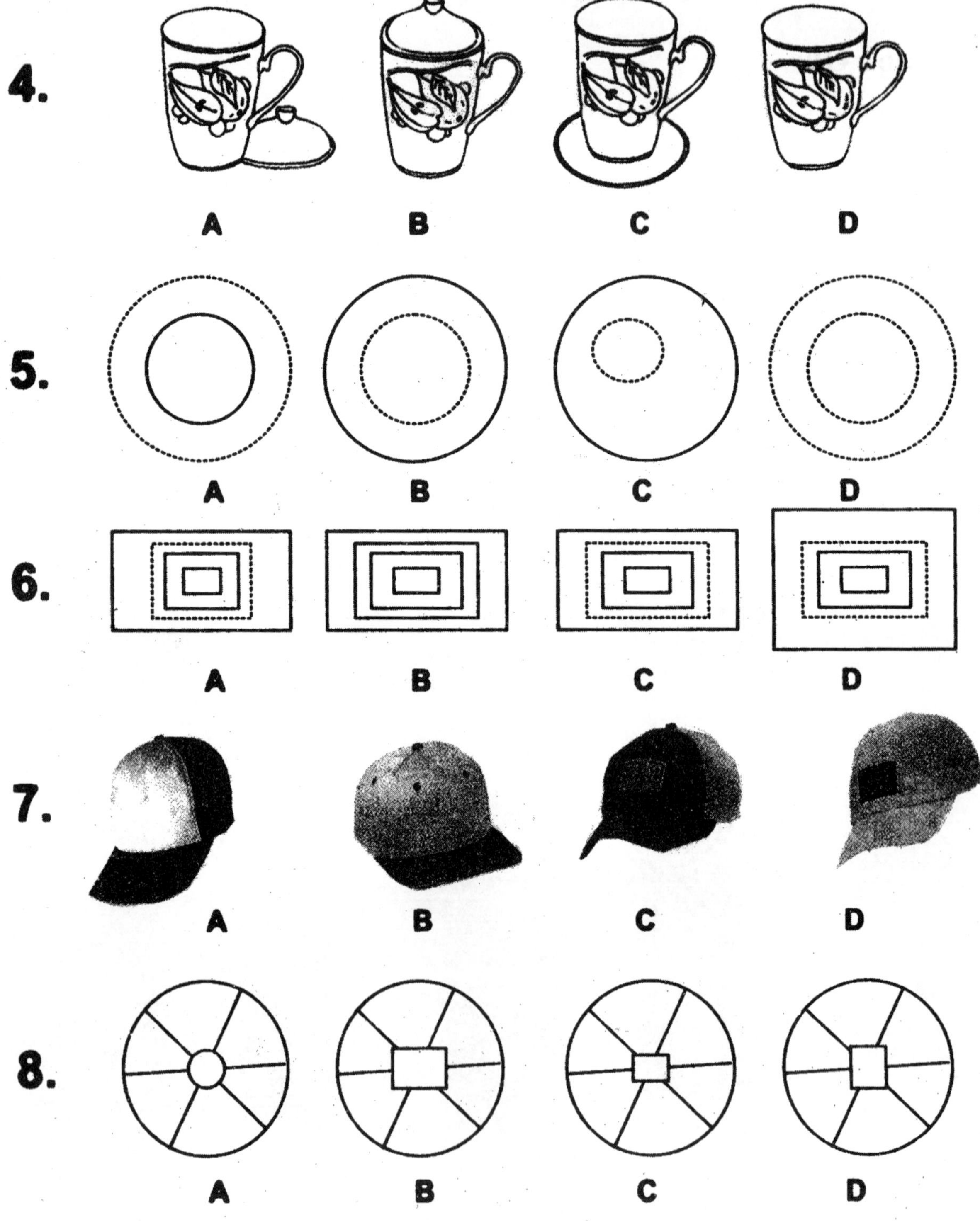
4.
A
B
C
D
5.
A
B
C
D
6.
A
B
C
D
7.
A
B
C
D
8.
A
B
C
D

International Tourism Management

Section Two

Complete this form by putting not more than three words for each answer in (9 – 17).

ITM: International Tourism Management course is a new course in the field of Tourism Management. This course not only includes teaching, research, industry expertise but also business **9.** ______________ Scottish Centre of Tourism provide expertise **10.** ________________ for teaching the students.

Opportunities: Students get opportunities like

- ✯ Planning and Implementation of tourism **11.** ___________________
- ✯ Thorough understanding of contemporary tourism **12.** ___________________
- ✯ Proper handling of **13.** _________________________ issues.
- ✯ Learn to get **14.** ______________________ and **15.** ____________________

Skills: Students will learn transferable skills like

16. ________________________

17. ________________________

Independent Learning Ability

Circle the appropriate letter from (18 –22).

Benefits

18. ITM can be studied

A. Full time

B. Part time

C. Both

19. ITM gives

A. Academic Qualification/Professional qualification

B. Professional Qualification/ Industrial qualification

C. Academic/ Professional/ Industrial qualification

D. Industrial Qualification

Subjects Offered:

20. ITM offers subjects like

A. E-business

B. E-business and IT application

C. Case Studies & Decision Making

D. All of the above

Career Opportunities:

21. An ITM candidate gets career in the field of Public Sector Tourism like

A. Leisure Organisation

B. Tourism research

C. Regional Tourist Boards

D. Visitor attraction

22. Customer Focussed Organisation gets

A. Leisure Organisation

B. Travel Organisation

C. Business Tool Kit

D. Tourist Research

Section Three

Listen the tapescript and lable the diagram from (23 – 29) recycling of aluminium. Write not more than three words for each answer.

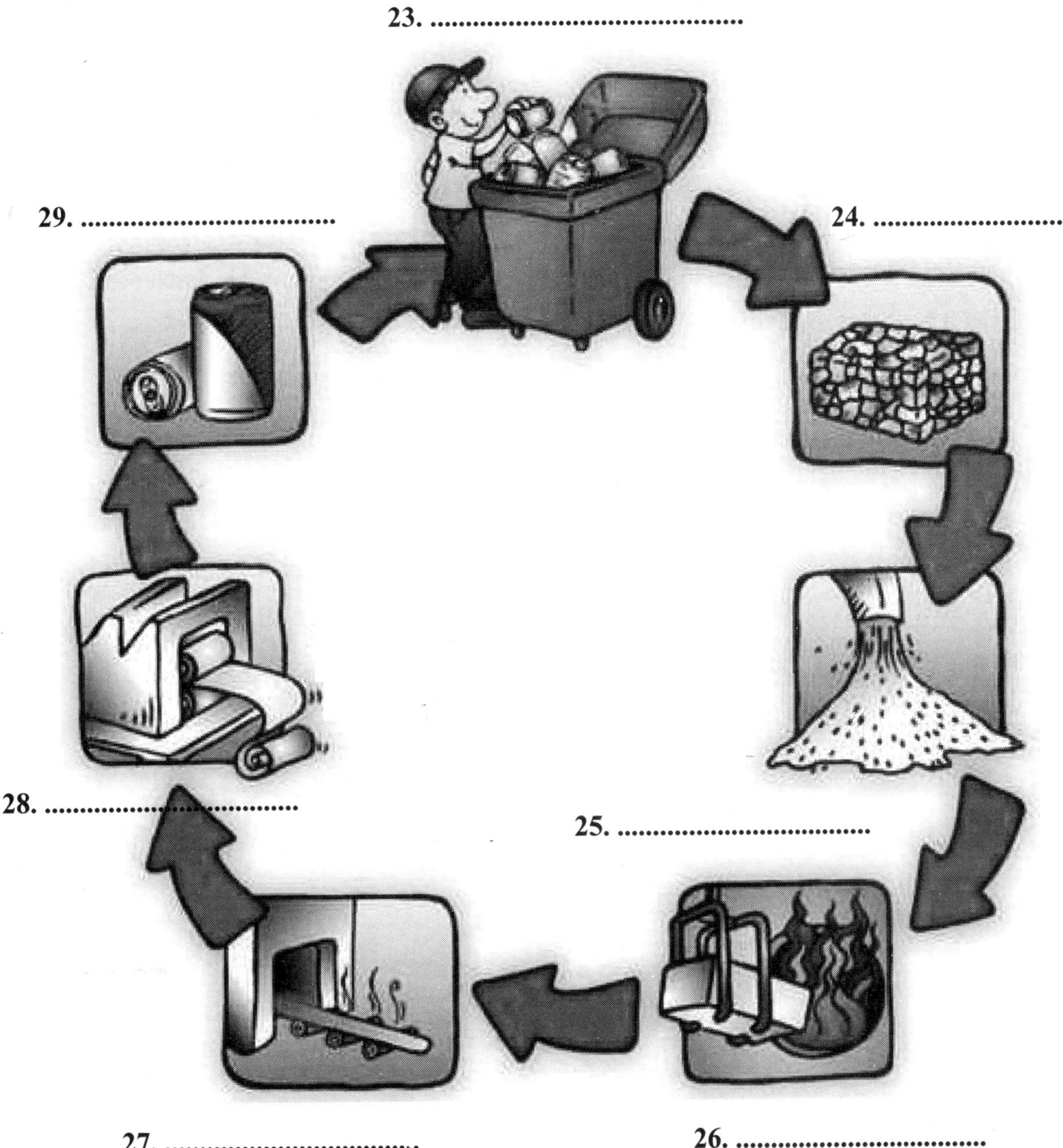

Recycling of Aluminium

Section Four

Complete the following summary from (30 – 40) by using words from the box. There are more words in the box than you need. Some may be used more than once.

rest	relaxed	angry	warm
stress	work	hunger	45 degrees
chew	exhaustion	desk	40 degrees
noise	tense	study	crowed
speak	smoky	relaxtion	long-term
tired	exercise	raised	

The most usual cause of headache is 30. ________________________ Headache can also come as a result of excessive 31. ________________________. Some people say they get a headache when they 32. ________________________. This is probably because they get very 33. ________________. It may also be because they are working in poor light which makes them very 34. ____________________. It is helpful if your reading material is on a book\rested at 35. ____________________ to the desk. It is also important to 36. ____________________________ in bed. You may even get a headache because you 37. __________________ too hard. The best advice is to try to eat regular meals, get enough 38. __________________ and avoid 39. __________________________ places. These places can also do you serious 40. _______________ damage.

Answer Sheet for Listening Test - 2

1.		**21.**	
2.		**22.**	
3.		**23.**	
4.		**24.**	
5.		**25.**	
6.		**26.**	
7.		**27.**	
8.		**28.**	
9.		**29.**	
10.		**30.**	
11.		**31.**	
12.		**32.**	
14.		**33.**	
15.		**34.**	
16.		**35.**	
17.		**36.**	
18.		**37.**	
19.		**39.**	
20.		**40.**	

Listening Total ________________

Listening Test 2

Answers

Section One

1. C	2. A	3. B	4. A
5. D	6. B	7. C	8. C

Section Two

9. Management Skills	10. Staff	11. Strategies	12. Issues
13. Complex	14. Autonomously	15. Professionally	16. Initiative
17. Decision-making	18. C	19. C	20. D
21. C	22. C		

Section Three

23. Unsed not thrown	24. Collected and Crushed		25. Large bale
26. Molten aluminium	27. Thin sheet	28. Punching of Cans	
29. Decorated and filled			

Section Four

30. hunger	31. noise	32. study
33. tense	34. tired	35. 45 degrees
36. relaxed	37. chew	38. exercise
39. smoky	40. long-term	

Listening Practice Test – 3

Section One

Listen the Japanese Culture of 'Go-game' and complete the following blanks from (1 – 10) by putting not more three words on your answer sheet.

1. OTHER NAME OF 'GO'

   ____

2. ORIGIN IN

   ____

3. INTRODUCED IN

   ____

4. IN CONTEMPORARY TIMES 'GO' IS AN

   ____

   ✯ Indoor game

   ✯ Outdoor game

5. In Earlier times 'GO' is an

   ✯ Indoor game

   ✯ Outdoor game

6. THEME OF 'GO' GAME ______________________
7. PLAYERS ________________________________
8. TYPES OF STONES ________________________
9. CAPTURING MORE TERRITORIAL MEANS ___________________________
10. People's Participation means _______________________________________

GO-GAME OF JAPAN

Section Two

Listen to the spectacular acts of White Elephants of Thailand devlivered by the narrator, and complete the following summary using not more than three words for each answer. Now answer the following questions (11 – 26) on your answer sheet.

WHITE ELEPHANTS of Thailand is a symbol of 11 ________________________ and 12 ________________________ . King of THAILAND is honoured with the hightest "Order of 13 __________________. Thailand white elephants are appreciated because of its 14 ________________________ on the field of sport foot movement, agility. Racing and tactics are the special skills of Elephants. By getting the signal of take off elephants 15.____________________ immediately. OFTEN Elephants are competitive. They play obstacle race elephants football, sparying 16. ________________ are quite common Elephants loved music. They are 17 __________________ in the rock Jazz and 18. ____________________ categories. By getting command from their trainer they sway and prance of the 19 _______________ trunk 20 ___________________ feet keeping time with 21 _____________________ and heads 22 __________________ Elephants are best friends they even have their 23____________________ and 24 _____________ Elephant's friendship becomes most obvious when the female is above ready to give 25 _______________ she solicits help in 26 _______________

Section Three

Listen to the tapescript and lable the process of paper making. Write not more than three words for each answer (27 – 31).

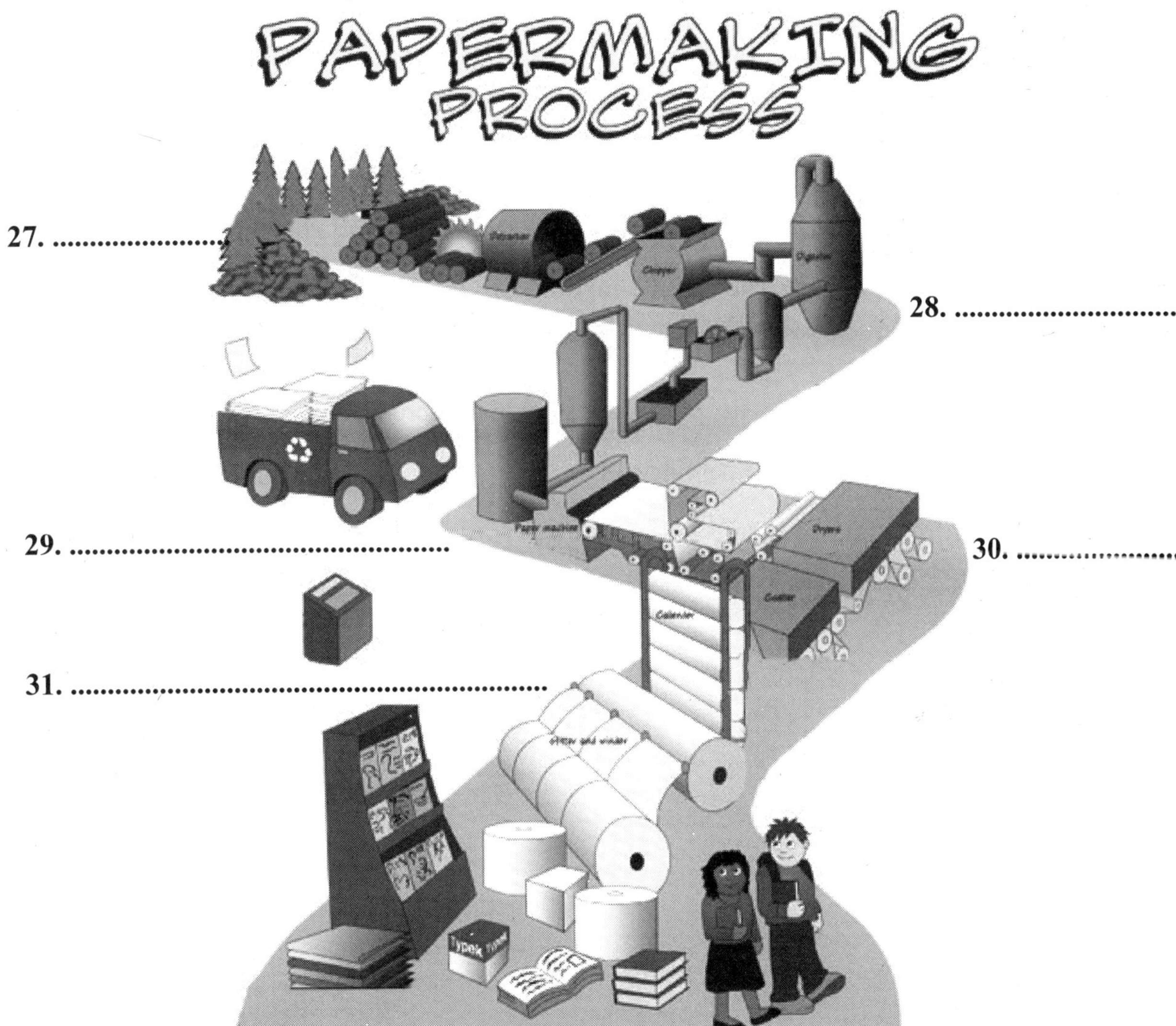

Section Four

This section willl tell you about the deatiled description of the process of paper making. Listen to the tapescript and complete the summary by using words from the box. There are more words in the box than you need. Some words may have been used more than once. Now listen carefully and answer the following questions (32 – 40) on your answer sheet.

25	Wire
Water	Wood
Trees	Finished
Web	Cooked
Bark	Dyes
Coatings	Logs

Forest product companies and 32. ___________ for paper making. In the process of paper making, debarker is used for removing 33. ______________ and chippers are used to cut the 34. ________________ Then in the mixture of water and chemicals these chips are pressure 35. _______________ . Later pulp is bleached and pumped into a moving 36 _____________ screen. When the pulp travels down the screen, 37. ________________ is drained away and recycled. The semidry 38. _____________ is passed through heated dryer to remove the remaining water. 39. ________________ paper is wound into large rolls whose weight is around 40. _______________ tons.

Answer Sheet for Listening Test - 3

1.
2.
3.
4.
5.
6.
7.
8.
9.
10.
11.
12.
14.
15.
16.
17.
18.
19.
20.

21.
22.
23.
24.
25.
26.
27.
28.
29.
30.
31.
32.
33.
34.
35.
36.
37.
39.
40.

Listening Total ________________

Listening Test 3

Answers

Section One

1.	Go/Go board game	2.	China	3.	Japan
4.	Indoor game	5.	Outdoor game	6.	Winning Territory
7.	Two	8.	black & White	9.	Winner
10.	Seven million				

Section Two

11.	Power	12.	Place	13.	White elephant
14.	Intelligence	15.	stampede	16.	water games
17.	trained	18.	folk	19.	rhythm
20.	Initiative	21.	beat	22.	to and fro
23.	likes	24.	dislikes	25.	birth
26.	Delivery				

Section Three

27.	Forestry	28.	Debarking, chipping/Recycling
29.	PulpPreparation	30.	Paper formation
31.	Paper finishing		

Section Four

32.	trees	33.	bark	34.	wood
35.	cooked	36.	wire	37.	water
38.	web	39.	Finished	40.	25

OLYMPIAD BOOKS FOR CLASSES 1-10

V&S Publishers, after the grand success of a number of Academic and General books, has brought out a series of Olympiad books for different classes under The Gen X series – generating Xcellence in generation X – which has been designed to ease the problems faced by students. In all books the concepts have been explained through examples, illustrations and diagrams, wherever required.

MATHS

SCIENCE

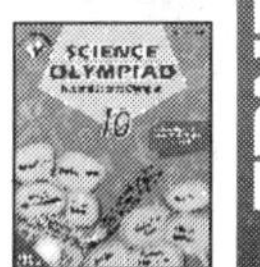

CYBER

Computer Olympiad

ENGLISH

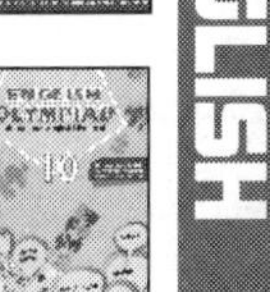

OLYMPIAD HIGHLIGHTS

- Study chart for systematic preparation
- Tips and Tricks to solve problems quickly
- Precise Theory explained with examples, illustrations and diagrams
- Multiple Choice Questions with Answer Keys, Hints and Solutions for practice.
- Higher Order Thinking Skills (HOTS) Questions to assess your skills
- Model Papers for real time practice before exams.
- Planners for understanding the pattern of Olympiad

OLYMPIAD PLANNER

While other books in the market focus selectively on questions or theories; V&S Publisher's Olympiad series is precise yet comprehensive. Each planner provides step-wise guidance to go through the exam i.e. how to register, tips and study chart for efficient preparation, pattern and syllabus of exam, recommended study material, and awards and scholarships.